Social Structure and Church Planting

Social Structure and Church Planting

A study of cultural concerns of the receptors of the Gospel

John E. Apeh

Foreword by Clyde Cook

"I wish I would have had such a resource for my students and myself many years ago ..."

— Clyde Cook
President, Biola University

To obtain copies of this book or for correspondence write:

Indigenous Missions International
P.O. Box 2498
Atascadero, CA 93423
U.S.A.

Prepared for publication by
Companion Press
P.O. Box 351
Shippensburg, PA 17257

ISBN 0-914903-85-3
Library of Congress 89-80200

For Worldwide Distribution
Printed in the U.S.A.

TABLE OF CONTENTS

FOREWORD

With this study Dr. John E. Apeh has made a significant contribution to effective church planting. As a former Professor of Missions teaching courses on social structure and church growth, I wish I would have had such a resource for my students and myself many years ago.

Dr. Apeh's theme in this work is, "that the church planter needs to be sensitive to the social structure of his receptors." The church planter "also needs to apply social structural insights to his church planting process in order that churches might be dynamically conditioned to their socio-cultural environments."

While there has been a growing awareness of this need, this study gives us a very practical and useable way to implement such truth.

Dr. Apeh comes with a wide background in ministry experience to address church planting in a cross-cultural setting. Although his case studies are specific and come out of his experience with the Igala culture, he has extracted general principles that can be applied to other cross-cultural church planting settings.

I feel the evidence has mounted overwhelmingly in the past fifteen years of the importance and crucial nature of social structure in church planting. Yet I wonder how much of this has filtered down and is being taught to missionary candidates.

This book meets a vital need for institutions of higher education that are preparing missionary candidates and church planters, as well as mission candidate schools in their pre-service programs. It is also a book that needs to be read by experienced missionaries and mission leaders, as it will make them more effective in both training those involved in this noble task, as well as helping them to implement these programs.

As more and more church planters are coming from the developing nations, to have such a monumental work by one of their own signifies a milestone in the carrying out of the Great Commission.

May God bless you as you grapple with these issues so eloquently stated by Dr. Apeh and may the Holy Spirit guide you to extract His truth from this study, which will help you plant churches that will grow qualitatively and quantitatively.

Clyde Cook
President
Biola University

Chapter One

INTRODUCTION

Since Pentecost (Acts 2) when the Holy Spirit came to inaugurate the Church, the planting of the Church of Christ has been an important task of the Christian body. God's instrument, the Church, has been active in evangelism, discipleship and organizing new believers into a local congregation.

Although much has been written on the subjects of evangelism, witnessing, discipleship and the doctrine of the Church, theological and missiological studies have not identified the need for a specific study of social structure for church planting.

Previous studies and writings on church planting have focused on important issues: the art of communication, the refining of the message and the development of the communication skills of the messenger. Bible colleges and seminaries function to train Christian missionaries in the Word of God — the message of the gospel — and to develop effective communication of the message. These training programs provide skills needed by missionaries to proclaim their message well. However, these have been at the expense and neglect of the social context factor which is essential to the planting of a church. The understanding of social structure is fundamental to effective church planting. Three reasons are advanced for this assertion: (1) social structure is exemplified in the New Testament pattern of the Church, (2) social structure is inherent in the church planting process and (3) social structure is foundational to contextualization of the message and the messenger.

Social structure is exemplified in the New Testament pattern of the Church

The significance of social structure can be seen in the Word of God. Some examples and cases in the New Testament show the importance of social structure of the church planting process of the early church. First of all, on the day of Pentecost (Acts 2), the Holy Spirit recognized the importance of using languages indigenous to the listeners present. As the disciples were filled with the Holy Spirit, they spoke in the different languages of their receptors (Acts 2:6). And that same principle stands true today: using the receptors' language is crucial to the understanding and reception of the message of the gospel.

Secondly, when there was a conflict arising out of the neglect of the Grecian Jewish widows (Acts 6:1-4) in the daily distribution of food, the Apostles recognized that socio-economic problems were significant elements in their ministry. Rather than denying the problem, or spiritualizing the situation, they decided to address the problem by ensuring that other believers full of the Holy Spirit take that problem as a ministry within the church. Acts 5-7 shows that their number increased; the church grew rapidly as people's needs (food) were ministered to.

Thirdly, the Apostles referred to early Hebrew history in their addresses. Peter used this method in Acts 2:1-36 by his reference to the prophets and Psalms. Only Jews familiar with the Old Testament would have understood what Peter was getting at. At his defense in Acts 7:1-55, Stephen relied on his understanding of Hebrew history in addressing the Jews. Similarly, Peter and James appealed to the Jews with the use of the Old Testament passages during the Jerusalem Council (Acts 15:1-29; 21:21). These passages show the relevance of history, ancestry and pedigree to communication. In these instances, references to the Law helped them to effectively communicate to their audience. They were sensitive to the culture of their receptors and did all they could to foster understanding and good receptivity.

Fourth, and finally, the Apostle Paul used social context factors of his audience, receptors, and companions to promote understanding, interpersonal relationships, and effective ministry in proclaiming Christ to both Jews and Gentiles. Indeed, he became all things to all men for the sake of leading them to Christ (I Cor. 9:22). Specifically, it should be realized that Paul was culturally sensitive to the Jews and Judaizers in Jerusalem. This could be seen prior to his arrest in Jerusalem and during his defense there (Acts 21:20-26; 24:10-19; 22:1-12; 23:6-8).

Paul was also careful in his dealing with the Judaizers who often accused him (Gal. 2:3-5, 11-16). Paul used his own knowledge of the Law effectively and used it to introduce the gospel of salvation by faith in Christ, although he was falsely accused of preaching against the Law of Moses. When he ministered to the Gentiles, he used what he knew about their background (Acts 17:16-24). Throughout the epistles of Paul to Gentile Christians, he reminded them of their former practices and the need to put on the new nature (Eph. 2:1-13; Col. 3:1-11; Tit. 1:5-16; Rom. 1-2).

It would seem obvious that social context factors are important if so many Scriptures are devoted to the issues affecting the receptors of the gospel message. However, it is regretful that contemporary church planters pay little or no attention to the crucial issues involved in the social structure of their receptors. This neglect or ignorance or both is capable of rendering the church planting process ineffective.

Social Structure is Inherent in the Church Planting Process

There are at least four factors inherent in church planting. They are the message, the messenger, the method, and the receptor. These factors, which are crucial to church planting, show that social structure is fundamental to that process; and church planters ought to acknowledge its importance and effectiveness for church planting.

Message: The church planter goes with a message. The content of his message is the good news of salvation by faith in Christ. But he must see to it that his message is separated from his culture. Burnett comments,

> Unreached people find it confusing to know what is the real message of the gospel as distinct from the particular culture of

> the messenger. A tribal person may consider the wearing of Western-style clothes as an essential mark of Christianity ... The only way this may be overcome is for the missionary to identify with the people in as many ways as possible (1984:50).

If he is to succeed, his message must be put in the context of his receptors. According to Cotterell, "the message has to be communicated across cultural barriers ... and we must be sensitive to (sic) the message which is to be transmitted and encoded" (1984:116). It is imperative that a cross-cultural church planter be able to understand what it means to separate his culture from his message and how to communicate a contextualized message to his hearers.

Messenger: The attitude of modern missionary societies toward social context factors can be seen in their internship and candidate school programs. It is common-place for mission agencies/boards to organize a two- to eight-week study for prospective missionaries anticipating cross-cultural ministries. Often this program of study involves only basic cultural information for the benefit and survival of their missionaries. While these training programs are commendable, they are not much more than survival kits for missionaries. And although they are exclusively designed to facilitate missionary entry into the receptor's culture, they are mostly taught by foreigners and individuals who have little or no field experience with the people the missionaries will be working with. They do not answer specific questions or the issues pertinent to the sociocultural setting of church planting.

To prepare prospective missionaries to not only survive but minister to their receptors, training programs must utilize the expertise of national believers and experienced and seasoned missionaries who have been successful on the field. Both the mission-sending agencies and missionaries must see the importance of social context factors on church planting and its ultimate effect on their outreach. The following case illustrates a social context problem often faced by church planters.

> A national elder was visiting a missionary one afternoon. Arriving on the mission station, he went to see the missionary with whom he had worked for many years. When he knocked

on the door, the wife of the missionary came out to meet him. Without exchanging greetings, she asked, "What do you want?" The man replied, "Nothing, I just want to see the owner of the house." The woman then told the man that her husband was asleep and that she would take a message for him. This elder left annoyed for three reasons: (1) without exchanging greetings she demanded to know why he was there, (2) according to custom, she should have asked him to come in and give him water to drink, then allow him to explain why he came, and (3) she expected the man to tell her what he came to tell her husband. To the elder this was improper, as he had nothing to do with the wife. It was the man that he had been working with and had no reason to relate to the woman. And because she indicated that her husband was napping, the elder concluded within himself that sleeping was more important to the missionary than he was. He further could not understand why the missionary's wife behaved this way, and this incident created a barrier between the national elder and his missionary friend.

The type of problem shown in this case is common on the field because of the difference in backgrounds of the church planter/missionary and his receptors. It is a problem of social structure basic to cross-cultural church planting, and it is the responsibility of the messenger to know what are the dynamics of his receptors' structure.

Method: The messenger uses a method in delivering his message, known as communication theory. Such theory must be appropriate if the message is to be understood.

According to Burnett,

> Our methods and practice must be culturally relevant. We must start with people where they are, and meet the needs that they feel ... All too often the missionary to the inner city is running a program based on suburban church patterns, with Sunday schools organized along structures only relevant for the middle class. Our church timetables, patterns of worship, and modes of evangelism must be relevant to the local church in which we are placed by God (1984:50).

It is crucial that the church planter realize this if he expects his message to be heard, understood and received.

Receptor: In addition to the need for an appropriate form of communication, the need for the church planter to relate his teaching to the issues confronting his receptors is significant. Reception of the gospel is the goal of the missionary, and receptors are the object of his ministry. For instance, teachings regarding full-time service and commitment should be preceded by a thorough analysis of the socio-cultural implications resulting from obeying it. The following case exemplifies cross-cultural difficulties in calling national believers to full-time service.

> Samson and John attended the same church until they were both called into full-time ministry. Both of them came from the same tribe, and were married with families to support. In addition, they were the bread winners of their extended family members which consisted of their parents, brothers and sisters.
>
> Soon after their call to the ministry, they began to experience some pressures from their families. By going into full-time service, they left their jobs without the consent of their wives and members of their extended family. Because full-time ministry promises no financial reward, it upset their kinsmen who had depended upon them previously.
>
> Samson and John, however, did not realize the serious implications of this economic problem and so did not pay attention nor care to address it. They were happy to have made commitment to their Lord in service. But they forgot that this act of commitment was regarded as an irresponsible act by their families.
>
> As expected, they were unable to discharge their social obligations, since they were no longer earning salaries. Their support was inadequate to supply the needs of their family obligations. It is ironic that no one told Samson or John about this problem before they decided to quit their jobs. Although they were being used to reach the lost, they lost opportunities to reach their immediate family members.

Had Samson and John realized the serious social and economic implications that their decision would have on their extended families, they would have prepared before leaving their jobs. This type of problem arising out of ignorance and insensitivity to social structure can be addressed by educating the missionary on the significance of social structure to church planting. The following principles serve as a guide to stimulating awareness of social structure and its importance to the church planting process. National believers and evangelists might find these principles helpful as well.

1. *Receptors must be reached with the gospel in an appropriate way.* If a missionary is to have a lasting impact among a people group not his own, he must identify social values and mores in the culture. For instance, a child was led to Christ. His family was furious and forbade him to attend church. Out of respect for his family, he obeyed. How would one advise the boy? In the chapters ahead, as we study cultural differences and family structures, an understanding of the receptor should shed light on the appropriate method to share Christ.

2. *Accurate perception of one's receptors is based on one's understanding of their social world views.* The common mistake church planters make is to assume what and how people are. We perceive people as we have been told. Knowing the social context, the people themselves would help us to gain a more accurate understanding of their ways. For example:

> A man came to visit a missionary at his mission station. The missionary was at the table with his family when the man came in. He was asked to sit in the living room until they finished eating in the dining room. He began to ponder why the missionaries behaved in such a way toward him. Culturally, the missionaries should have asked him to join them at the table. And in response, he is customarily expected to refuse the invitation since he did not come there to eat. But even when he refuses, the missionaries are expected to persuade him to eat.

By ignoring cultural parameters, the missionaries lost the trust of this man, who misinterpreted their behavior and took offense at their rejection. And because they were ignorant of the cultural practice, they assumed his mealtime visit was purposefully to beg food from them. Misunderstandings beginning at this level are exemplary of the rift in communication that occurs without the necessary foundation of acculturation.

3. *Indigenous leadership patterns must relate to their social context.* Before a mission advances its organizational methods and principles, a study of the people and their leadership patterns is warranted. Organizing believers into a local congregation necessitates the selection and appointment of leaders. The steps taken to install a culturally and biblically based leadership must be in agreement with the practices of one's receptors.

4. *Issues of discipleship and theological agendas which must be Bible based ought to be issues which are of significant interest and concern to the people.* Training and curriculum must be contextualized; systematic theology also must address issues crucial to the people in their social context. In this way, biblical Christianity becomes relevant to people's life experiences.

5. *The application of the message depends largely on an understanding of the receptors.* Therefore, understanding social context factors is as important as the message and communication methods. Church planters ought to spend a considerable amount of time studying the social context in which they serve. This will greatly improve their understanding of the appropriate cultural communication methods as well as how to apply the gospel message. Even national believers may fall into the same snare. For instance,

> when I was a sophomore in college, a young man came as a freshman to the college. He had previously lived in the United States for about four years. He was a very nice young man, but he had just returned to Nigeria and had forgotten some of the cultural expectations. Once, when he was eating, he asked some of the students, "You wanna eat?" The students responded that they did not, and the Americanized student accepted their response without question. It was not until later that he discovered why they had turned him down. First, he used American slang when he spoke to them. To the students, he was trying to show off that he had been to America. Secondly, the students came from cultural backgrounds where it was wrong to ask whether somebody wants to eat when one is eating. To these students, the custom is to say, "Come and

> eat." If they did not want to eat, they would have responded that they were satisfied or full. By asking whether they wanted to eat, it was taken to mean that they really desired to eat and that he was not really ready to share food with them. In this case, the student relearned the proper cultural responses.

The example shows that people are not discriminating on the basis of one's race but, rather, the foreign element exhibited through practices, life styles, and personal and interpersonal communication.

What a church planter says is important. Equally important are nonverbal communication styles. The case below shows how the lifestyle of a church planter may speak louder than his voice.

> Summer missionaries from the United States came to one mission to work. They were well received by the church and community. A few days after their arrival, some of the women were seen wearing slacks. They were also repeatedly seen with the male teammates engaging in behaviors such as hugging and sitting on each other's laps. In the afternoon the women changed to shorts and sleeveless T-shirts in order to get a suntan. The nationals saw them in all these acts, and were surprised by the appearance of immorality among those who came to preach the gospel.

It is important that the church planter be conscious of his actions before his receptors. The impression one leaves with national believers may be different from the intentions of the church planter. This is because of the differences in their cultural backgrounds. It is for this reason that efforts should be made by the church planter to relate and identify with his receptors in order to minimize such differences and potential conflicts.

Social structure is foundational to contextualization of the message and the messenger

Contextualization is the process of putting a message into appropriate language for the understanding of its receptors. In relation to the gospel and theology, it is the process by which the recipients of the gospel and theology are brought into an understanding within their own context and setting. This process takes into cognizance three principles which are necessary in bringing about such understanding (see Table 1):

1. Social Context of receptors [People]
2. Cultural Communication method of receptors [Form]
3. Relevant Content [Content]

The issue of social context of the receptors is important because it has to do with people whose world views are diverse and changing within time. And because the receptors' form or method of communication is also diverse and changing, contextualization becomes constant with the social context.

However, the content of the gospel does not change. The form of its proclamation will change with developments in the social context and cultural communication method. While the content of systematic theology which is based on issues of interest to receptors changes, the Bible remains the source of all theologies.

Contextualization is as complex as the people group targeted by the missionary. Any communicator who is an outsider needs to operate an appropriate strategy of communication, teaching and training.

The purpose of this book is to communicate how social structure undergirds the divine directive of cross-cultural church planting. Receptivity, spiritual growth and development of the church depend on a proclamation that is sensitive to the social structure of the receptors of the gospel message. This book identifies and applies such social context issues that are significant for church planting and recommends their use by cross-cultural church planters for effective proclamation, discipleship and organization.

The issues of research in social structure discussed in this book are the issues of economics, structure of relationship, marriage and family, social activities and hierarchies, kinship, political leadership and contemporary social changes and dynamics of the people among whom a church is planted. These social issues examined in this book provide a framework to which strategies for church planting should relate.

Drawing on research of the Igala people of central Nigeria, this in-depth study sets the framework for enhancing ministry across cultural barriers. While most of the illustrations used may be limited

Table 1. **Church Planting and Contextualization**

Areas of Contextualization	Elements of Church Planting	Factors of Church Planting	Principles of Contextualization	Principal Focus
Gospel	Evangelism →	Church Planter/Evangelist	Communicator/Teacher	Message and Messenger
		Message (Gospel)	Content (Gospel)	
		Method (Communication theory)	Method (Cultural Communication Form)	Cultural form of Communication
		Receptors (People to be reached)	Social Context (People and their culture)	Appropriate to the receptors
Systematic Theology	Discipleship and Organization of Congregation →	Church Planter/Teacher	Teacher/Leader	Message and Messanger While message and content of Bible does not change, messenger is limited by his own culture.
		Message (Biblical/Systematic Theology)	Content (Bible and theology)	
		Method of Instruction and Organization	Indigenous Method of Instruction and Structure of Organizational leadership	Revelant content is determined by receptors'social context factors based on issues of significant concern to them. Biblical content does not change, but issues of concern to receptors are added to content of systematic theology.
		Believers/Church	Indigenous believers	

to this culture, principles have been extracted to offer insight into social structure and the international church planting process. Further, the examination of the Igala case shows the implications of social structure for the national church planter, evangelists, and others involved in cross-cultural church planting process. It is my objective that the principles derived from the Igala case would prove effective among other cross-cultural missionary settings. It is also my objective that this study may serve as a tool to guide God's messengers into a more fruitful ministry to people groups throughout the world.

Chapter Two

HOUSEHOLDS AND ECONOMICS

Evangelism for church planting targets households. A household may consist of a family head, a wife or children in one or more separate families, lineages, clans, tribes, or different nationalities and races. Whatever role the receptors play, their family structure creates the contextual environment for evangelism. The church planter should recognize the importance of family structure and domestic life. He needs to know what constitutes a family and the social strata within the household. It is important that he understands the specific roles and functions of each member of the family. The church planter can become thoroughly acquainted with his receptors by asking questions which apply to their situation and practice.

CONTEXTUAL MISSIOLOGICAL QUESTIONS

For the church planter to understand his receptors, he needs to know them well. Questions concerning households and economics are appropriate toward understanding the social context of church planting. And though the data upon which the answers are based may change, the following set of missiological questions can aid church planters in understanding their cross-cultural settings.

(1) What is the structure of family life like in this culture and how do the members function to sustain the structure?
(2) How is this structure different from my own culture? What essential features separate it from my own?
(3) What are the specific cultural roles of each member of the family in this culture and how important are the role distinctions to the people?
(4) What things should I as a church planter consider in relation to the family life of my receptors and how can I work with their own system to introduce what I believe to be biblical and necessary principles for a healthy church life?
(5) What cultural elements in the family structure need to be confronted with the Bible and how am I going to introduce it without offending my receptors or being considered ethnocentric?
(6) Am I really allowing my receptor's culture to be critiqued biblically or are my own cultural values getting in the way?
(7) What economic pursuits are my receptors involved in; how can I understand their economic life?
(8) How do they respond to economic pursuits differently than spiritual pursuits? Why the difference?
(9) What sex role distinctions do I notice in economic pursuits and what things do people tend to spend their time on?
(10) What is the importance of land, crops and ancestry to the family and economic lives of my receptors? What are the major economic interests and contemporary changes noticed in their economic system? How do they respond to changes in economic, religious and household activities differently?
(11) How are the issues of leadership and bread-winning roles in the household and interpersonal relationships crucial to indigenous church leadership, financial contributions to church ministries and church fellowship?
(12) How are decisions made in the household and what type of leadership style is it? How different is the leadership style in economic activities and how do people relate, unite, compete and interact?

CASE STUDY: IGALA HOUSEHOLDS AND ECONOMICS

The understanding of households in relation to those being reached with the gospel is crucial to discipleship and leadership organization. In training and teaching ministries within the church context, there is need for a thorough understanding of relationships, roles, functions and expectations of individuals represented. For example, the Igala people define relationships in the household in terms of three social statuses: the family head (husband), the wife and the children. The specific role definitions for these statuses create the distinctive structure of Igala domestic life.

ENE'NYI, "HEAD OF THE HOUSE"

In Igala culture the man is the head of the family. He is called the *Ene'nyi,* literally the "owner of the house." As the owner of the house, he is expected to be in charge and in total control. When the *Ene'nyi,* "head of the house," exercises control, he is judged to be a "real" man, *One'kele de,* but when he shows weakness, people refer to him as *Onobule,* woman. If he wants to be respected as a man, he must remain in control and must not allow his wife to dominate him.

The social role of *Ene'nyi* includes the following obligations, rights, and privileges:

1. He is expected to provide for his family.
2. He is expected to make decisions for the family.
3. The wife or wives is/are responsible to him.
4. The children are directly responsible to him.
5. He is responsible for the acts of those in his family.
6. His decisions are never challenged.
7. The wife and children are his properties.
8. The wife and children do not have private properties while under the authority of the head of the family.
9. He is the chief executive officer and the public relations officer.
10. He is the liason officer between the family and extended family members in the community and as such cannot be represented by the wife or female children.

The head of the household holds power over the members of his family and demands their respect. However, in return he is responsible for providing his family's needs.

As the head, he has the authority to decide on the number of wives and the number of children he wants to have. It is also his responsibility to establish a good extended family network upon which his family members relate to their extended family members, *amomaye kpai efu ma.*

In political matters the husband and father is the one who decides what is most proper and advantageous for his family. He decides for whom the family should vote in an election and what party is appropriate. While the members serve his interests, he too serves their economic interests by supplying their daily and special needs.

The head of the household is the spiritual leader as well. It is his responsibility to organize and offer sacrifices on behalf of the family. In such religious matters, he delegates responsibilities to his wife (wives) and children with regard to the procurement of items or materials for sacrifices and rituals. For instance, during religious festivals, he calls upon his wife or wives to purchase and prepare locally brewed corn wine with the produce or money he supplies. While children may take part in this festival, they obey and take direction from their father.

Clearly, the Igala household and family structure is patriarchal. When the head of the family dies, he is buried by his own brothers or paternal cousins and relations. The children and wife have nothing to say about such burial arrangements. His widow could be taken in marriage by any of his relatives to perpetuate his name.

OYA, "THE WIFE"

The wife is the woman of the house or *Oya, onobule-unyi* in Igala. As the woman of the house she is expected to obey her husband in all matters, bear and rear children, cook, participate in harvesting crops and entertain guests and be hospitable to extended family members. Igala men look upon women as weak and dependent people. In terms of physical maturity, they are considered little more mature than children.

The social role of *Oya*, "wife," includes the following obligations, rights and privileges:

1. She bears as many children as possible and rears them.
2. She listens to the husband in all matters.
3. She ensures that food is available on the table at the right time.
4. She harvests crops from her husband's farm.
5. She keeps a small garden where pepper and vegetables are grown.
6. She plants pepper and vegetables on the family farm in a specially designated area.
7. She provides all ingredients for food apart from the main food items (it is considered an insult for a woman to rely on her husband for such ingredients as pepper, spices, salt and vegetables).
8. She controls the female children completely.
9. She controls or employs the male children in the evening or late afternoon (the day of the male children belongs to the head of the family).
10. She takes care of all cooking and washing of dishes (the female children assist her).
11. She makes sure that water is always available in the pot for her children and her husband.

The predominant forms of women's roles in Igala culture are the household and domestic affairs. Her responsibilities are so great and burdensome that it is impossible to expect her to fulfill outside roles if she is to be an effective, consistent, and good housewife that her husband will trust and retain. In most cases, in social matters, she is to be seen, participate, cooperate and see that the family works as a unit for the glory of the husband. She must submit her own economic interests to her husband.

In political matters, Igala expect women to support their husband. Women may campaign among women folk only for the husband's candidates or political parties. Politically active women organize social festivals to support their husband's campaigning and fund raising toward the husband's political goals and objectives.

Igala expect a woman to have her own god and to be very religious, but she is not to be vocal in spiritual matters of the household. In the family, she is to cooperate with her husband in meeting the needs of the household gods or deities. She cannot lead in prayer or sacrifices, *ichebo,* but she can prepare food needed for *ichebo* and other offerings.

A man expects his wife to abstain from extramarital sexual affairs and she is not permitted to have men friends. The husband is, however, free to maintain concubines and take more wives with or without the wife's consent.

She has no say in the number of children she can have. The will of the husband is her own will. In most cases this will continue for as long as she can reproduce (as long as God provides). The more children a woman bears, the greater her bargaining power or source of influence with her husband or favor from him.

Finally, a woman is always an "outsider" in her own household. The land, household, children and products of her labor are owned by her husband. Until her death, she is the property of her husband. When she dies, her body is taken by her own kinsmen. The husband and children have no business in the location of her burial.

AMOMA, "THE CHILDREN"

Igala regard children as blessings and gifts of marriage. The more children a woman bears, the stronger her security in marriage with her husband.

Responsibilities and expectations for children vary on the basis of sex. While the father, as the head of the house, is the sole authority and expects everyone to report to him, male children have a more direct relationship to him and as such, have unique responsibilities. Female children report directly to their mother but give indirect account to their father. Female children, *amoma onobule,* and male children, *amoma enekele,* bear distinctive responsibilities which harmonize the family structure as a single entity.

The role of male children *(amoma enekele)* includes the following expectations and rights:

1. They are expected to work on the father's farm during the day until they reach marriageable age.
2. They are expected to work on their mother's farms in the evenings (late afternoon) until they reach marriageable age, *oko ane.*

3. They are to remain close to their father in order to observe, learn, and become familiar with their roles, their rights and their responsibilities to other members of the family (mother, sisters, younger brothers).
4. They assist their father in social, political, and spiritual matters.
5. They alone have the right of inheritance which is patriarchal and patrilineal.
6. They are responsible to perpetuate the family line, i.e., bear as many children as possible to keep their father's line/name going. They can marry their late father's wife (not their mother).
7. In the absence of the head of the home (father) they preside at family meetings (especially the first born) over the mother and elder sisters.
8. Even when they marry and have their own family, they are expected to live with or close to their parents.
9. They are to provide all needed security for their parents when they can no longer provide for themselves (parents are brought to live with them or they move to live with their parents). There is no nursing home and it is considered a shame and disgrace to the male children to allow the female children to take custody of their parents.
10. They are responsible to provide for all their younger brothers and sisters until they are old enough to fend for themselves. In the absence of the father, they work hand in hand with their father's brothers in giving away their sisters in marriage.
11. Though they have the right of inheritance, if they are underage when their father dies, the paternal relations assume the administration of the deceased estate until the children are of age to inherit whatever is left.
12. When their widowed mother or step mother desires to remarry, their approval must be sought. This is especially true if she is to remarry somebody who is not the deceased's kinsman.

The role of *amoma onobule* (female children) is limited to supporting their mothers and learning the essentials of the female role. Whatever responsibilities are placed on them must be relinquished at marriage — when they formally become part of another (their husband's) family. Until the female children are married, they are required:

1. To help their mother in all domestic activities.
2. To help the family and especially to cooperate with their own brothers for the good name of their father.
3. To refrain from premarital sexual activity for the sake of bringing honor to the father's house.
4. To be industrious and have the ability to cook delicious meals so that they are not an embarrassment to the mother when they marry.

Unlike the male children, they inherit nothing — all ties to the family are broken at marriage.

Although technically speaking a female child is no longer part of her father's family at marriage, she has the right to return if her husband mistreats her and does not provide for her. Her parents and brothers see to it that she does not regret or suffer at her husband's home. Ties to her father's family can be maintained by giving one of her children to her father or brother to raise. And when she dies, she is returned to her family for burial. Her husband and children have no say in this arrangement.

Parents expect children to be in submission in all matters. Parents arrange marriage for them. When they are not arranged, they must have the approval of their parents and kinsmen. As children, they are thought to be too immature to face life.

In turn, the children provide for their parents when they are grown — a power exchange takes place between parent and child. When the children are grown and the parents are still young enough to provide for themselves, there is a joint effort of sharing within the family. But as old age hinders the parent from activity, the child takes on the provider role, and the power shifts. Still, the authority of the parent remains intact: Igala greatly respect their elderly and are obligated to provide for them.

The issues of family, responsibility, respect for the elders and the importance of cooperation and unity in the household all form the mold for developing an effective discipleship and leadership training program. These bases of family structure are tools which reach out to the community which the church planter targets. But reaching people individually or corporately must be utilized with sensitivity and respect for the way tradition dictates. Many times Christian workers have turned parents against their children or husbands against their wives by their ignorance and disregard for the structure of Igala households.

In the interest of church planting, Christian workers should avail themselves of the tremendous benefits in observing cultural norms and traditional institutions.

THE DOMESTIC ECONOMY

How people make their living should be of considerable interest to church planters. Christian missions are guilty of neglecting the economic life of those they reach with the gospel. The nonspiritual aspect of people's lives is seemingly unimportant to Christian missions. Yet to divorce the spiritual from the physical needs is an unbiblical stance. In the guise of conservativism, Christian missions opposed to a social gospel have remained adamant to social concerns.

The economic life of those being evangelized, discipled and shepherded has serious spiritual implications. Understanding what receptors do and how they make their living is significant. Furthermore, the dynamics of their economic activities, methods and use of their resources have great significance to the life of the church. It is necessary for a church planter to identify with his receptors in what they spend most of their lives doing. Such physical identification enhances his witness and ministry. For example, the Igala people are involved in a number of different economic activities. In all of these activities, the roles of men and women follow two predominant themes. Igala allocate most of the "production" labor to men, and the "processing" tasks to women and children. Because the men control both production and produce, they hold power over the women and children who are involved in the processing sector (see Table 2).

The men are involved in three main subsistence activities. These are farming, trading and dressing and selling of fruits. Farming involves land clearing, cultivation, sowing/planting, weeding and

Table 2. OCCUPATIONAL DISTRIBUTION

TYPE OF LABOR	MALE	FEMALE	CHILDREN
Cooking		XXX	XX Female children
Harvesting of crops	X	XXX	XX
Land clearing	XXX		XX Male children
Cultivation	XXX	X	XX " "
Sowing/planting	XXX	X	XX " "
Weeding	XXX	X	XX " "
Dyeing	XXX	X	—
Load carrying	X	XXX	XXX
Fetching of water		XXX	XX
Construction of houses	XXX		X Male Children
Cutting/hauling of firewood		XXX	XX Female children
Buying and selling of groceries		XXX	XX " "
Selling of cash crops	XXX	X	
Cutting of palm fruits	XXX		X Male children
Brewing of corn wine		XXX	
Tapping of palm wine	XXX		X Male children
Palm oil processing		XXX	X Female children
Palm kernel processing		XXX	X " "
Plaiting of hair		XXX	XX " "
Hair oil processing		XXX	XX " "
Hunting	XXX		XX Male children
Grave digging	XXX		X " "
Soap making		XXX	X Female children
Driving	XXX		
Mechanic/repairs	XXX		XX Male children
Government jobs	XXX	XX	XX all
Hawking	XXX	XXX	XX

XXX - Full and active participation
XX - Marginal participation
X - Occasional participation

dressing of orchards. Trading involves the actual selling of cash crops such as maize, beans, melon, rice, corn, etc., while the business of taking care of palm trees, okra trees, cocoa, coffee, cola nuts and locust beans are the exclusive responsibilities of the men. The women's role in relation to these activities is to process whatever is produced by the men through their various subsistence activities. And because women are looked upon as weak people, they cannot be involved in strenuous activities such as is common in production processes.

ECONOMIC INTERESTS OF FAMILY

The Igala people have a great economic interest in their land, *ane,* orchards, *oli ero,* and cash crops, *oje kitoko.* It should be realized that Igala consider lands and orchards as an inheritance from their ancestors. This is very crucial to the way the Igala venerate their ancestors because their very existence depends on things inherited from them. To continue to hold onto the ancestors' inheritance, they must continually venerate them. They believe that the ancestors will inflict sickness on them if they do not do so. This can be illustrated in the case of Iye.

> Iye was a poor man who lived on subsistence farming. Although his grandfathers were landowners and had a good supply of economic trees on their farm land, Iye had nothing to claim because another powerful clan had taken over his inheritance. One day, he decided that he must fight for the land. He had seen how much money those who took over his grandfather's lands were making from palm trees and okra trees.
>
> After venerating his ancestors and consultations through the *Ifa Oracle,* he claimed that he was assured by his ancestors that the land would be given back to him. On this assurance he instituted a civil action in a court of law. He took a loan to pay for legal fees and other expenses. He was to repay the loan after the case was won and the trees were harvested and sold. Fortunately for Iye, he won the case and became the rightful owner of the land with all the trees. However, the land customarily belonged to Iye's family since he is not the only grandson.
>
> At the end of the court case, he forgot to venerate his ancestors and to thank them for giving him victory and protection from the attacks of the defendants. He became seriously ill. The opponents (defendants) had threatened that

he would be killed for taking away the land from them. He consulted his relatives and extended family members and they in turn consulted the *Ifa Oracle.* Then it was determined that the illness was caused by his own ancestors for failing to offer them a blood sacrifice. On realizing that, Iye's family organized a blood sacrifice and ritual ceremony to venerate his ancestors. After this ritual, he became well and his ancestors pledged continued protection from the defendants.

In this case, it can be seen that people fight for economic interests. They are constantly defending themselves from the attacks of their enemies who are jealous of their success and possessions. In the same way, they enjoy good health as well as their families if they venerate their ancestors. These dynamics are basic for economic interests and survival. In Iye's lineage, there continued to be a family feud over who should control what and how to share the inheritance of their common ancestors.

IGALA TECHNOLOGY

The Igala employs cultural knowledge in producing certain needed goods. These goods are for both domestic and commercial purposes. Participation in these economic activities is based on age and sex. In Igala technologies, the men are involved in most of the commercial activities while the domestic needs are produced by women. The following are different types of indigenous technologies in which the men, women and children are involved respectively.

The Men

The men are involved in producing baskets, wood carving, black smithing, weaving of mats, granaries and fans. They are also involved in the weaving of grass roofing sheets and the preparation of herbal medicine. These activities are important because they bring in more income as well as help in meeting the needs of people. For instance:

Agba, "baskets," are used in carrying loads from the farm.
Uloko, "mats," are used as blankets or outdoor sleeping bags.

Aka, "granaries," are used to store harvested crops.

Upepe, "fans," are used to freshen the air during hot weather.

Alo, "black smithing," produces agricultural tools and implements.

Ojokunyi, "grass roofing sheets," are used to roof houses.

Ogwu, "herbal medicine," is used for the prevention and treatment of diseases.

The Women

Igala women are involved in producing at least three main items: corn wine for drinking at social meetings, soap (for washing), and hair oil for hair dressing.

Women are allowed by men to engage in these three areas of production because they do not involve any real physical activity which is regarded by men as strenuous. It should be realized too that corn wine is a product of corn which is planted and cultivated by the men. Table 1 shows that women are responsible for the harvesting of crops, including corn. While corn wine production may be believed by women to be in the production sector, the men are rightly the ones involved in the actual production of the raw materials. The same thing can be said of the soap and hair oil production which uses palm branches and pods as raw materials, since palm branches are cut down by the men.

Thus, women can be seen to be very active in subsistence and cash economics. However, their roles are limited and restricted to those activities that the men consider to be less strenuous.

The Children

The children are primarily involved in helping their parents. The male children are especially fond of weaving baskets, fans, and mats, while the female children enjoy brewing corn wine.

CHANGES NOTICED IN THE ECONOMIC SYSTEM

Before the coming of Western education, about 95% of the Igala were involved in agriculture as their main occupational activity. With the coming of Western education and industrialization, a number of changes occurred. As industries were being established in the cities, many went out in search of factory jobs. Some of those who remained in the villages went into non-traditional occupational activities.

Most Igala farmers, however, remained very orthodox and were skeptical of the modern system of mechanized agriculture. The government tried unsuccessfully to introduce mechanized farming to them and the use of fertilizer (pre-1974). But the decline in agricultural production, the rise of food prices and the mass importation of food items led the government to rethink its methods. The Igala people believe in their own system. It is the only way they know. And because most of their people cannot afford the economic implications of mechanized farming, it is very hard for them to believe that the new system will be able to serve their interests.

The introduction of public cooperative farms by the government contradicted the traditional society in which land was vested in families and lineages. Though the government did not study the implications of the new system, they did anticipate potential conflicts with the old. Instead of forcing the people to consider the more effective and alternative method of farming, officials bought tractors and fertilizers and established demonstration farms in many communities (between 1974-1977). This was done to show the people the difference between their own traditional method and the new method. The government also subsidized the cost of fertilizer and fixed the rate at which tractors could be hired so low so that many farmers were attracted. Gradually, officials succeded in convincing the farmers that while the new method was different from the previous method, it was more effective and profitable.

In Igala society today (since 1978), most farmers use tractors and fertilizers because they can produce much more than the normal subsistence farm. Though the government has stopped subsidizing the cost of tractors and fertilizers, many farmers continue to support the new system because it is fast, reliable and helps them to maintain a sizeable farm. They were willing to change because of the economic advantages of the new system.

The demonstration farms helped people to believe that the new system could improve food production. This belief changed the people's traditional world view.

APPLICATION: IMPLICATIONS FOR CHURCH PLANTING

There are at least six crucial issues here which are of significant relevance to the church planter in Igala family structure and its domestic economy. These crucial issues relate to authority, leadership, interpersonal relationship and stewardship in the church.

Authority, Power and Control

The head of the family, *ene nyi*, has the power to control his household and, in return for his absolute authority, he is the responsible provider for his house. The Igala church should be sensitive to this world view when dealing with selection and appointment of leaders for the church.

An understanding of the Igala household structure is crucial to the way the church is built and organized. The authority of the head of the family may determine the growth or decline of the church. It is important for the church to know that by combining different households in a church, the authority and power factors are bound to create tension. Furthermore, where the church cuts across family, lineage and clan barriers, every effort should be made by the church to appoint a balanced and diverse leadership who represent amiably the family structures existing within the body.

Contextualization of scriptural principles amidst family structures can be another source of tension in the church. I Timothy 3 and Titus 1 contradict the cultural leadership pattern of the people. This tension and conflict must be recognized and kept in focus by the church.

Sex Roles

Roles are well stratified between the men, women and children. In assigning responsibilities in the church it is very important to recognize that one's sex determines the type of responsibilities to be assigned. In ministering, sexual stratification should be respected by the church. The egalitarian teaching of the liberal theologians must be evaluated in the light of the Bible and Igala culture. Issues such as debate over women's roles in theological circles must be weighed with the Bible and Igala world view in focus.

Age Stratification

The special emphasis on age differentiations needs to be considered by the church in relation to leadership and outreach ministry. The young people are considered unwise and as such cannot lead the older people. In the same way, care should be taken in outreach ministries to ensure that the young people reach their own age group while the older people are encouraged to reach their own group. The Bible recognizes the potential conflict between the old and young, especially when it comes to matters of leadership.

Relationship

Relationship existing among Igala family members is very intimate and strong. The church should capitalize on this when reaching the Igala with the gospel. Instead of the emphasis on person to person evangelism, it is advisable to evangelize the Igala by families, since the head of the family can greatly influence the decision of the other members. Even where young people are specifically targeted, they should be encouraged to seek the permission and approval of their family authority.

It is important to realize that the Igala family structure is strong on unity, corporateness and obligations. This must be understood by the church in dealing with the subject of stewardship and Christian service. In teaching stewardship and giving, it should be recognized that the Igala people have a lot of extended family and family obligations. These obligations to other people by Igala Christians might be recognized as part of giving or stewardship. And, a fuller grasp of the financial support structure among families will help the church and her missionaries to understand her members, especially if they do not give satisfactorily.

In relation to full time Christian service, the Igala Christian who is considering such service faces the pressures of family members and relatives because of his social obligations to them. By going into full time service, he might not be able to fulfill these obligations. While everything should be done to encourage the Igala Christian for the Lord's work, the church should not put undue pressure on such a person. Alternately, the church must stress the importance of supporting Christian workers so that they can still fulfill their obligations to their people. Serving the Lord does not excuse them from honoring or discharging their obligations (see chapter 3 for extensive discussion).

The Importance of the Ancestors

Because most people are farmers and depend on farm lands and orchards, their ancestors who passed to them the property rights remain very important to them. Veneration of ancestors, though traditionally practiced in worship and respect, is not the prime motive of these landowners. They seek economic prosperity and view veneration of their ancestors as a means to that end.

Those involved in economic activities not directly tied to farmlands and orchards rely on the ancestors for protection, good health and prosperity. Their membership in a family and lineage depends on a common ancestor and such memberships are crucial to inheritance, kingship and social acceptance.

If the church must succeed in getting people to think less of their ancestors, she must work out alternative ways for meeting people's economic interests. Perhaps, the church might be able to help by getting involved in a holistic ministry with the view of helping the people to develop their skills and increase their productivity.

Responsibility

It is important that the church develop a theology to address the Igala household in the area of relationships, respect for the elders and the role of individuals in his or her family. Such theology will enable the church to influence the Igala family and possibly utilize gains from such teachings in evangelism and discipleship.

Chapter Three

VILLAGE, CLAN AND LINEAGE STRUCTURES

STRUCTURE OF RELATIONSHIP

People's relationship affects their attitudes and actions towards one another. In societies where people place value on corporate relationship, interaction, and integration as opposed to individualistic and nuclear societies, the nature of relationship existing between different people affects their response to the gospel. Group response, interest and action are important elements in face-to-face societies, and those involved in church planting should be able to understand the group dynamics.

The village is the center of human activity. Living patterns within the village generally reflect the structure of relationship and its nature. The church planter needs to know what is significant in how people relate to one another and how they live. He needs to know why people tend to live together based on clan, lineage and family lines. The importance of land and how it unifies different families and lineages within a clan system is also crucial in understanding the dynamics of relationship and its application in church fellowship.

Every society has its own social security system and kinship system. The kinship system is significant to church planting because kinship ties also define relationships and social obligations.

In church planting it is important to realize how people work together, and why and whether kinship ties have any impact on the fellowship in the church. The receptors' social security system needs to be understood. Do people respond differently to their social obligations as opposed to church responsibilities? What differs? What is important to people considering full-time service in the church? Who are those involved in decision-making and why? What is the extent of influence one's kinsmen can have on his decision? These questions are helpful to those involved in church planting; they are crucial to the examination of the Igala society with its complex structure of relationship and must be taken into consideration when planting a church.

CONTEXTUAL MISSIOLOGICAL QUESTIONS

Like the households and economic systems of a people, their structure of relationship based on village, clan and lineage pattern is crucial to church planting across cultures. The church planter, in a society where such structures exist, should familiarize himself with relevant contextual missiological questions which will help him to fully understand his receptors.

Furthermore, issues of inheritance, right of ownership, extended family obligation, full-time ministry and social security system must be carefully observed and responded to properly. Because of the differences that may exist between the Igala practices and beliefs and those of others in which the church planter works, it is necessary that general culturally-sensitive questions relevant to the above issues are asked by the church planter in his own context.

The church planter needs to ask the following relevant questions appropriate to his receptors in his bid to know them and respect their own way of life.

(1) What is the structure of relationship existing in this culture, and how does this structure work? How does it help build relationships and foster strong kinship ties?

(2) How do people define tribe, village, clan, lineage, extended family and family units and what are the unique features of these units? How does the structure of relationship define how people should relate to themselves, to others and to foreigners?

(3) How do people settle and what are factors determining settlement patterns? What lesson can be learned to influence the location of the church in a village?

(4) How should the church be organized to incorporate the different relationships and accommodate everyone without violating rules of relationship and social activities? Can different villages, clans, lineages or tribes be brought together? Are they better off on a homogeneous principle?

(5) On what bases should leadership positions be filled; clan, tribe, village or lineage? And what role should sex (gender) and age stratifications play in such decisions?

(6) How should the Christians respond to their extended family members and to those with whom they have no blood relationship? How can the whole family, lineage, clan or village be reached or should evangelism focus on the individual? What is the best way to reach out without disrupting the family relationship and yet be fruitful?

(7) To whom should the new Christians owe allegiance; the church planter, their family, their church or to God, and how should the question of obedience to one's parents and to God be handled in a conflict situation?

(8) To what extent should the Christian teaching on separation be applied to one's extended family members who are still unsaved?

(9) How would you respond to those who need security in order to answer the call of God for service in keeping with their social obligations to their family members?

(10) In a society where people tend to live together on kinship bases, what should the church planter who needs to establish a boarding Bible School, move pastors from place to place, or remove Christians to his mission station do?

(11) Considering the weight of social responsibilities on national believers in an extended family system, what can the church planter do to avoid imposing his own concepts of individualism and nuclear family on his converts?

(12) What type of help can the church planter provide for the national believers who have definite needs without succumbing to paternalistic tendencies in relating to them?

CASE STUDY: IGALA VILLAGE, CLAN AND LINEAGE STRUCTURES

Certain Igala terms, central to Igala social organization, provide the framework for description and analysis in this chapter. The terms *amichi-one*, "tribes people," *abo ewo-one*, "one's village people," *efu-olopu*, "clan relatives," *amomaye-one*, "one's extended family," and *unyi-one*, "one's family" describe the structure of relationships in Igala society (see Figure 1). These forms are also used by the Igala in defining relationships between people on tribal, village, clan, lineage and family lines. Furthermore, they are factors determining the use of Igala kinship terms and the administration of social security obligation.

It is significant to realize that village, clan and lineage structures depend on the nature of relationships for survival and harmony in Igala society. In urban areas where Igala people are unable to trace relationships, unity, cooperation and interrelationships are hard to forge (see Chapter 6 for more details).

ICHI, "TRIBE"

The term *Ichi* refers to members of the same language group. Bilingual Igala translate this concept as "tribe." However, tribe to the Igala does not mean one culture, as people hold different beliefs and practices within the same tribe, *ichi*. Igala look at other Igala as *ene-omune*, "a different person."

To this category of people, the usual Igala hospitality is extended. The Igala concept of hospitality may be seen in the proverb, *"eju ononojo majome, ubiwn mara"* which means that the Igala will extend himself to make visitors/strangers feel at home even if it means taking a loan to do that.

Before other non-Igala people, an Igala person would introduce another Igala person as his own kinsman even though they may not be related. This is especially true of Igala people working in cities and towns outside the Igala area.

However, this *abo-omune*, "other Igala people," who are either from the same or different village may be looked down upon. They may be suspected or regarded as inferior non-relatives. In making this distinction between one's family members and other Igala non-relatives, the Igala would ask questions in relation to:

FIGURE 1: STRUCTURE OF RELATIONSHIP

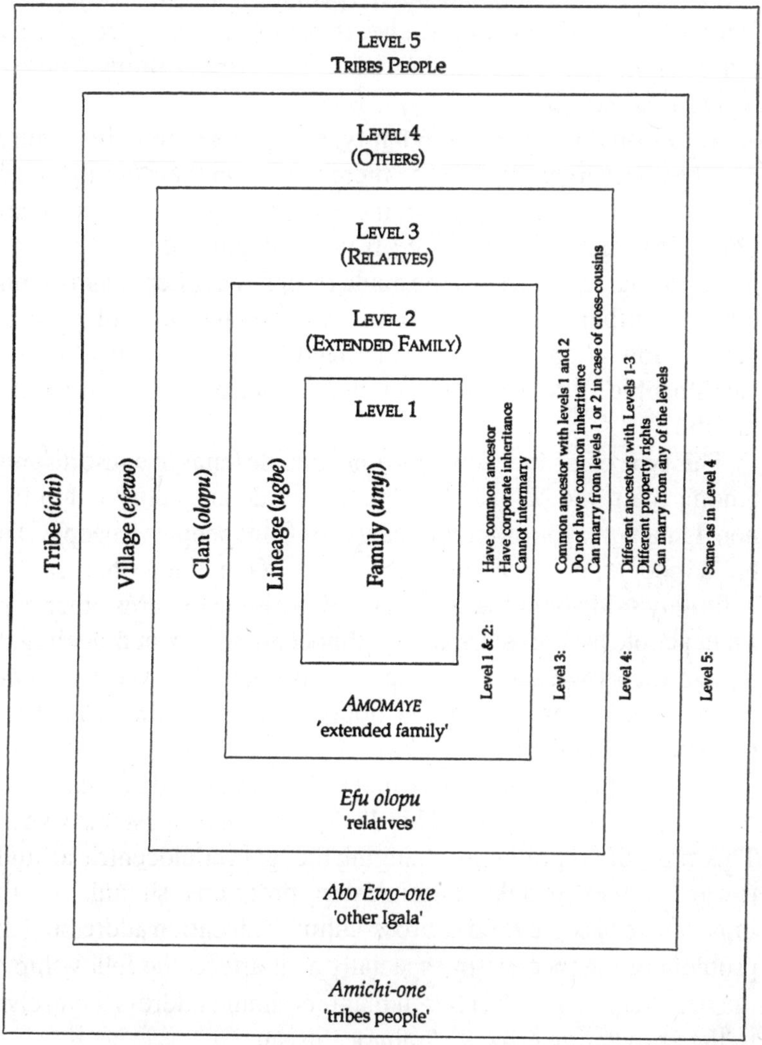

1. Lineage — What is his ancestral background, *abo ugbo de*? Who is the father and grandfather, *ene chata wn*? Where did they come from, *ugbo ma kwo wa*? What was their occupation, *ewn chichanama*?

2. Status — In relation to others, people often ask: Who is he, *ene iche*? What does he do, *ewn yache*? Is he and his family from a royal family, *amo ma ofe mache*? Were his grandparents brought here as slaves, *adu ma che*?

3. Personal Conduct — What type of people are in his family? Are they very industrious? Are there thieves in their family? Have they suffered from God's judgment (in the form of thunder and lightning)? Have they suffered from contagious disease(s) in the past? Special reference will be made to leprosy, epilepsy and mental illness. Further questions will be asked in the area of personal habits. How about food? Does he feed his family well? Are they clean people? Are their children under control? Are their women faithful?

This type of attitude towards other people tends to cause disunity among the same people. The Igala attitude and relationship to a non-Igala person is different and varies from people to people. The Igala people may be very hospitable. One thing that can be definitely said about them is that their attitude towards other non-Igala people is characterized by ethnocentrism. Even though Igala realize their own short-comings, it has been observed that other people's practices are looked upon as incompatible with Igala practices and beliefs.

It is important to emphasize that urbanization and secularization have exposed the Igala to all kinds of people in the past thirty years. This exposure is gradually changing the Igala ethnocentric attitude towards other people. Discipleship programs should see the importance of some form of cross-cultural education addressing the problem of ethnocentrism especially as it affects the fellowship of the believers. Similarly, church planters should address themselves to the devastating effects of ethnocentrism.

EFEWO, "VILLAGE" AND IGALA SETTLEMENT PATTERNS

An Igala village may contain several clans. Figure 2 illustrates the village of *Ofugo* in which the Igala people settle together as a

FIGURE 2: A SKETCH OF *OFUGO* VILLAGE SHOWING CLAN AREAS

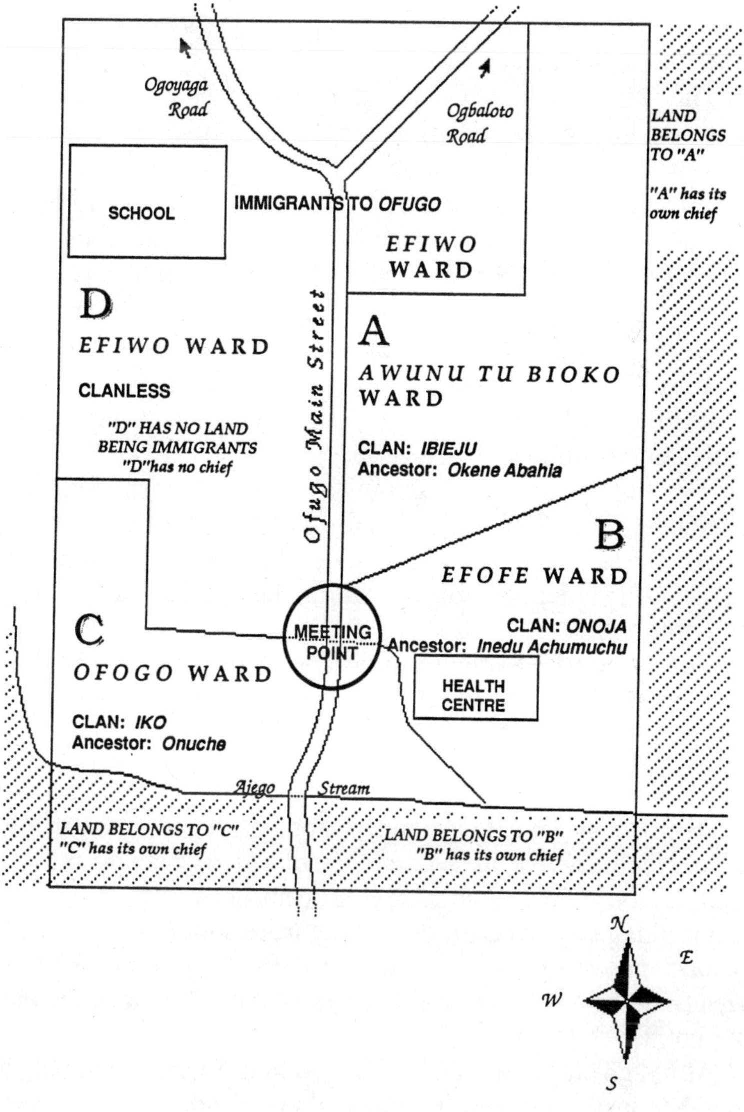

clan with well-defined territorial and geographical lines. Within a clan, *olopu,* are several extended family members who are members of the same lineage, *ugbe.*

The sketch of *Ofugo* shows four clan areas known as wards. Different lineages occupy their respective clan areas or wards. In the same way, different families occupy the portion that belongs to their lineages. The main determining factor in the allocation of land portions to lineages and families is where one's ancestors lived, worshipped, farmed and/or were buried. These four factors are very crucial in determining the location and size of land that can be allocated to lineages and families. Thus, in a clan area or ward, proximity of one to the other is first on family, second on lineage, and third on clan basis. The closer one's relationship, the closer the settlement location and vice versa.

The immigrants to *Ofugo* (Ward D) are considered by the original settlers (Wards A, B and C) as clanless because they came from different clans not indigenous to *Ofugo.* This means that they have no title to landed property within the *Ofugo* village and have no right to rule.

This pattern of living arrangement enables them to hold onto their inheritance tightly. It brings the family households together and forges unity as their corporate interests are protected.

OLOPU, "CLAN"

Olopu, "clan," means a group of people with a common ancestor. Clan members live in a common village or occupy the same community. People of the same clan do not necessarily live together in onc villagc, but whcrc they do, they share common territory. The Igala clans and lineages are patrilineal descent groups. The rule of agnatic descent recognizes a man's sister as one in his descent group but not her children.

Although clan members have a common ancestor and may live together in the same community, they do not have a common inheritance. They do, however, cooperate in religious, political, and economic activities. Usually, relationships on clan lines are stronger than those of tribal or village affinities.

UGBE, "LINEAGE," AND OWNERSHIP OF PROPERTY

Ugbe, "lineage," literally means seed. Members of a lineage stem from one common male "seed." In a clan there are many lineages; in a lineage there are many families. The number of families in a lineage depends on the number of children of the founder of a particular lineage. Igala classify members of a lineage who are not family as *efu*, "far relatives." The concept of *efu* classifies the relationship existing between different families from the third generation members of a lineage and beyond.

Property rights are vested in lineages. These rights are mainly over lands and orchards of palm, okra, coffee or cocoa. Because families make up a lineage, properties are shared among different families on a patrilineal and seniority basis. Such properties are corporately owned. This right to property is called *ewn ogwu*. Whenever a relative or family member dies, his properties will be inherited by his brothers.

Inheritance is patrilineal based on the adelphic principle. Only the Ego's sons can inherit their father's property: Ego's daughters are automatically excluded. Though Ego's sons are qualified, Ego's brothers are next of kin, and Ego's children can only share after the Ego's brothers have either taken their own share or voluntarily allowed Ego's son to inherit. Similarly, while Ego's brothers only can inherit Ego's property, Ego's fathers or father's brothers cannot descend so low as to inherit their son's property. The son can only inherit has father's property in the absence of his father's brothers. In the same way, Ego's wife cannot inherit her husband's property unless Ego's brothers specifically designate. Ego's children are the property of Ego's family, and Ego's wife has no say whatsoever. The concept of private ownership is foreign, as most things are jointly owned. Land is corporately owned and vested in the lineage. Lands are inherited from one's past ancestors. The economic interest in inheritance is so great that it usually undermines the loving care that the family of the deceased requires. The compelling economic interest in inheritance often threatens cooperation and corporate identity of families and lineages.

Igala believe that ancestors confer inheritance and property rights upon the living and remain a vital force to be reckoned with in daily life. The living must esteem and respect ancestors from whom land and prosperity come. The power of the ancestors is great, and it is possible to lose property rights if something foolish is done that brings ridicule to the ancestor's lineage or family.

AMOMAYE, "EXTENDED FAMILY"

Amomaye, "close relatives," includes members of the same family and of different families of the first and second generations. Thus, one's parents, brothers, sisters, parent's brothers and sisters, one's grandparents and their brothers and sisters and all the children in the above mentioned families are considered extended family members.

These Igala concepts define social identities which are central to the daily life of Igala people. The village is the primary residential unit. Within villages, people relate to one another according to distinctions of clan, lineage or family identity. This chapter addresses in detail the arrangement of family structure. A pattern illustrating lineage and relationship arises out of Figure 3.

It is the practice of the Igala people to extend mutual support to members of the extended family and help them in time of need. The obligation of taking care of the immediate members of the husband's family falls on the wives, who are under instruction from their husbands to fulfill their familial responsibility.

In the same way, a man also has the obligation to provide economic assistance to his parents-in-law and their families. And if he does not do what is expected of him, his parents-in-law will remind him.

Igala society judges those who refuse to take such responsibilities as irresponsible and bastard — an infidel and an outcast who will be looked down upon (vagabond). Such people have no influence in the community. To be regarded as such in the Igala society is equal to one who is deceased — dead, worthless, of no earthly value.

Extended family groups are significant in economic cooperation in the society. The main area of this is seen in the exchange of

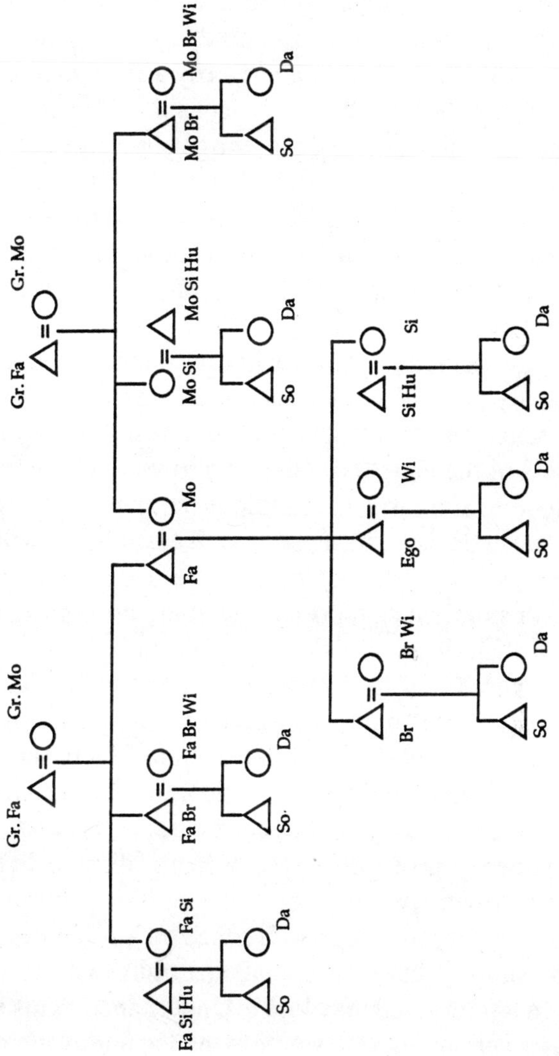

FIGURE 3: IGALA EXTENDED FAMILY

children to help in some economic activities. For example, a son sends his daughter or son to his grandparents or parents to be raised and to provide help for them. Similarly a sister can send her son or daughter to either brother, cross-cousins or her own parents and grandparents in order that they might be helped. These children may or may not be involved in economic activities.

Loans are also obtained from wealthy or rich relatives for any chosen economic activity. This is very common as it is believed that it is better for a member of one's family to enjoy his riches than a complete outsider.

In Igala society, extended family plays an important role in community politics and decision-making. It is the practice of the clan, lineage and family leaders, who are also the elders, to call all members of the clan to discuss who to vote for and what political party to join. Similarly, if a candidate happens to be from their clan or lineage, a decision to support such a candidate will be taken. In this way, support and legitimacy are acquired and maintained. Quest for political support can preclude any spiritual interest, so strong is their desire to hold political office.

In the same vein, decisions not to support a particular candidate by kin groups are on the basis of the relationship existing between their own clan and the candidate's clan. Where there is a cordial relationship, there will be solid support. In the absence of a cordial relationship, the reverse will be the case.

Extended family is also a factor in any dispute. In the event of a dispute involving two or more clans, settlement or support for legal action necessary for a redress is based on kinship ties. Anyone who fails to support his own extended family will be ostracized or declared a traitor and may lose his inheritance rights in his lineage.

This is perhaps an area where extended family members are very strong. Most kin groups have divinities thought to be the god of that family, lineage or clan and to which all members in that kin group owe allegiance. This is especially true of the Ancestors' Cult. The eldest son in the clan is the leader of a group that is known as "Sons of the Ancestors' Cult," *Amoma Egwu Afia.* Participants are expected to be responsible for *Ibegwu* rituals, the upkeep of the *Okula* Shrine and the keeping of all fetishes and utensils used in the Shrine.

It is difficult for a member of this type of clan to be converted to Christianity, as he has a strong kinship tie to his group. Very often pressures are put on potential converts and they are thereby inhibited from accepting a new religious system. Because people need kin support, protection, good health, and credibility for inheritance, they will cooperate and behave responsibly in this regard; they will resist the gospel. The church planter needs to understand and recognize the importance of extended family structure to its members. The introduction of the Christian faith should strengthen the extended family structure and enhance it rather than destroy the rich heritage of the people.

KINSHIP TERMS

In defining rules for relationship and expectations and obligations for such relationships, Igala kinship terms must be understood. These terms give specific and significant meaning to the nature of relationships of individuals to one another. The terminology is explained in Table 3.

Kinship ties are a major source of support in Igala. It is normal for one to get the backing and support of his own kin and those of affinal relatives. However, economic and political support depend largely on one's age, sex and type of relationship.

On the other hand, one is likely to face opposition from his kinsmen and women when he violates the rules or norms of the clan. This is especially true of people who act like vagabonds and are a source of shame and disgrace to the whole clan.

TABLE 3 **IGALA KINSHIP TERMINOLOGIES**

REFERENCE	ADDRESS	CATEGORY OF RELATIONSHIP
Okwo	*Atai*	FF, MF
Okwo	*Iyei*	FM, MM

TABLE 3 **IGALA KINSHIP TERMINOLOGIES**

REFERENCE	ADDRESS	CATEGORY OF RELATIONSHIP
Ata	*Baba*	F
Omaye Ata	*Baba*	FB
Iye	*Oja, Mama*	M
Omaye Iye	*Oja, Mama*	MS
Achogba-enekele	*Enegbani*	B (one's elder brother)
Okekele	*Oduwn*	B,Z (one's younger brother/sister)
Achogba-Onobule	*Iya*	Z (one's elder sister)
Omehi	*Omehi*	FZ (Father's sister)
Omenyi	*Baba*	MB (Mother's brother)
Oma, children	They are all addressed by the personal names	S, D, BS, BD, ZS, ZD, FBS, FBD, FZS, FZD, MBS, MBD, MZS, MZD
Oko	*Enenyi*	H
Oya	*Onobule*	W
Aju	Personal name	Grand S and D, SS, SD, DS, DD
Emaji	Personal name	Great Grand S and D SSS/D, SDS/D, SS/D,DDS/D
Omora	*Omaye*	Half sibling
Ana Onekele	*Baba*	WF, WFB
Ora-Oko	*Baba*	HF, HFB
Ana Onobule	*Oja*	WM, WMZ, WFZ
Iye-Oko	*Oja*	HM, HMZ, HFZ
Onigbo	*Onigbo*	HB, HZ, HZS, HZD
Omaye oya	Personal names	WB, WZ

Respect for elders can be seen in the way the young are expected to address the elders. Children are called by their names, and one is also free to call all those younger than themselves by their names. The young, however, cannot call their elders by name. They must use the appropriate terms given in the above table.

Igala kinship terminology is characterized by bifurcate merging (Murdock 1949:104) in the parent's generation. For instance, mother's sisters are classified as one's mothers. Similarly, one's father's brothers are considered one's fathers, and obligations of relationship in such cases must be in terms of child-parent expectations. The consequence of this is that an Igala child has several adults who may provide care and discipline as a parent.

The nature of Igala kinship should be an incentive for church planters to minister to groups in families, lineages or clans. Thus, instead of focusing on one individual, the kinship system provides an opportunity to reach the whole or many members of the groups involved.

SOCIAL SECURITY, *"OGWU UDU-OMUNE"*

In Igala culture, what is referred to as social security is looked upon as a family obligation or *adukidukpe kone ane.* This social obligation which rests upon families and members of each family are in relation to the following people:

1. the widow, *oya ukwu oko*
2. children of the deceased, *amoma yiokwu*
3. the elderly, *abogijo*
4. the handicapped (physically and mentally,) *abo kuma choga*

Oya-ukwoko, "the widow" — The responsibility of providing for the needs of widows rests with the family members of the widow's deceased husband, both immediate and extended, *amomaye eneyioku.* Other relatives, *efu* in the lineage and clan usually provide some support, but they are not required to because of the distance of their relationship to the deceased. Igala also practice the levirate system in which the widow becomes the wife of a surviving male family member. If she refuses to marry one of the family members, she must not remarry. If she remarries, she must leave the deceased's house completely.

Amoma Yiokwu, "children of the deceased" — The brothers of the deceased by custom inherit the children of the deceased. Because the widow has no right over her children, it is the responsibility of those who inherit the children to raise and provide for them. If the deceased's children are matured, they remain in their father's house to take care of his house and family members. They also must provide for their mother. However, the son's provision for their mother does not free their father's brothers from their own obligations. They are only free when the widow decides to remarry outside the deceased's family.

Abogijo, "the aged or elderly" — The elderly are well-respected and provided for. It is the responsibility of the children to take care of their aged parents. It is the Igala practice for the first male child to live with his parents in the same compound. This arrangement helps him to assume automatic responsibility and leadership as soon as the parents become too old and inactive to lead or to provide for themselves. Other children, male or female, are expected to assist their elder brother in caring for their aged parents.

Where the male children have separate homes or live in different locations, they either relocate to be very close to their parents or move their parents to live with them. The female children are not allowed to take ultimate responsibility as long as the male children are alive.

In the case of a family where the male children have all died or where there are no male children, the female children will arrange to take care of their parents. Usually their husbands will allow them to bring the parents to their house, but only if their own brothers and sisters are dead. It is a shameful practice for one to live with his or her son-in-law when he or she has a family who could assist.

The handicapped, the physically handicapped, *abo kuma choga,*, and mentally handicapped, *ama himu,* are cared for by their parents, brothers and sisters and other family members. This is an obligation. No one should be left to die by himself or herself. In the case of mentally ill people, efforts are normally made to confine them to their compounds. However, when they become uncontrollable and nothing else can be done to help them, they are allowed to wander in the streets.

It should be realized that these social security measures are part of the extended family obligations. This same obligation is placed on the elder or eldest members of every family by their younger siblings. In the same way, the care of the wife of any of the family members, in the absence of the husband, is the responsibility of those left behind.

Elder men in a lineage gain power through the survivor rights to widows and children. It is economical to have one's deceased brother's children help on the farm. The power to control the labor of a widow is another interest. The surviving brother gains prestige or honor for fulfilling his obligations to the deceased; it shows his credibility. In the same way, the power of the men to control women can be seen in the care for the elderly. Male children usually do not allow their sisters to remove their parents to their sister's matrimonial homes. It is an insult to the male children and to the brothers and sisters of the parents. These interests — respect, prestige, credibility, and desire to show one's responsibleness — often lead to the desire to control and maintain tradition.

APPLICATION: IMPLICATIONS FOR CHURCH PLANTING

The Igala village, clan and lineage structures are very important and ought to be taken seriously. Some of the issues the church planter must look at carefully include the following:

Inheritance and Right of Ownership

The concept of private ownership is new in Igala society. In traditional culture, whatever a man inherits does not belong to him and his children alone. It will surely be passed on to another member of his family when he dies. In fact, his very wife belongs to his family and any interested member of the deceased family can marry the widow. This also applies to the deceased's children. The church planter should use this practice to teach Christians that what they possess or own belongs to God; and that they are responsible to the Lord for how their resources are used.

The fact that corporate or group ownership is practiced should be an encouragement for the church to teach the importance of sharing liberally among the brethren. It should be emphasized that in Christ we belong to the same family or lineage so that the mentality of private ownership or division should not be allowed to cripple the needed unity and fellowship in the church.

Landed property is very important to the Igala people. Everyone living in his own village has a piece of farm land in his possession.

Land owners are highly respected since it is a symbol of power, control, respect and wealth. It is also a symbol of right to a particular village and its authority structure. The church should bear this in mind when pastors or full-time evangelists are posted to villages or towns other than their own. Such church workers will not be respected and may not influence people because as strangers they have nothing to symbolize power and authority.

Social Security System

The care for the widow, orphan, elderly and the handicapped are obligations imposed by tradition. The church planter should encourage the believers to be faithful to this tradition. This is especially important because of the principle of inheritance which seems to favor the brothers of the deceased instead of the children and the widow. Since the church is not in the position to change the law of inheritance, she must teach the Igala Christians the importance of their social security system if they want to maintain a credible Christian testimony to the unsaved.

Respect for Elders

Respect for elders, as seen in the form of address by the young people, should serve as an eye opener to the church to consider the place of the young people in the ministry. It is obvious that young people may not function well in a society that does not respect their age, wisdom, and ability. While the church should be meticulous about spiritual qualifications, she should also be sensitive and considerate in this area.

Extended Family and Full Time Ministry

Sociological factors inhibiting the growth of missions must not be taken lightly. These factors are in relation to one's extended family members. For instance, when an Igala Christian is called into full-time service of the church, the decision to honor the Lord's call is not left exclusively to the individual or his nuclear family. The one who is called must also discuss his call to full-time ministry with his extended family members, and the impact of one's call to ministry on his extended family members is great. Because he is expected to provide for his own family as well as those in his extended family, the decision to quit his job (where support comes from) and to take on a church ministry (which has little or no strong support base) is bound to create tension, anxiety and conflict.

This is especially crucial in a situation where one's extended family kinsmen are not Christians. Even if one's kinsmen are mostly Christians, there is often conflict arising out of their own concept of commitment to Christ and its experience. Tension exists also among Bible school students who face opposition from parents, friends and extended family members because they have chosen a ministry vocation which may not bring in economic benefits. Igala hold a poor view of ministry because of the stereotype of church workers who always seem to be among the lowest paid workers in Igala society.

The church has a responsibility to change this perception and belief. Igala Christians must be well taught to support God's servants who labor among them. The fact that one answers the call to full-time ministry does not constitute an oath of poverty. Furthermore, in view of the economic problems facing the Igala church, it is important that the church introduce an integrated training program to provide adequate theological and vocational education to those called into the ministry of the church. Such an integrated training would help provide the support church workers need as they are equipped with trade skills and can therefore support themselves as they minister. The strict traditional theological education in which ministers are trained for the church may be ideal, but it is inconsistent and irrelevant to the sociological problems that the Igala church and Christians face and to which they must relate.

Similarly, the belief or understanding of some Igala Christians that theological studies necessarily constitute call to full-time service, that such theological school graduates must be automatically absorbed into service by the church, and that a salary must be paid ought to be addressed adequately by the church. While it is biblical to support all those in the Lord's work, there is nothing in the Bible which says that the church must hire all theological graduates. Furthermore, theological school graduates could as readily engage themselves in self-supporting vocations. Full-time service is a privilege for believers, and support for such service is the responsibility of believers. However, both the serving and supporting brethren must see their respective roles as a privilege that should never be allowed to a resort to servant-master relationship. Full-time workers must not be a burden to the church nor present themselves as the church's liabilities.

Many of the issues raised in this chapter are the same in most West African societies. Despite the danger of generalizations, the importance of drawing principles and conclusions from these issues is a valuable effort which applies to any situation where church planters have to face traditional institutions.

Chapter Four

THE INSTITUTION OF MARRIAGE

The law or statutes of marriage vary from culture to culture. Even within the same culture rules regarding marriage may be different. Christian missionaries often face difficult problems handling marriage matters in cultures other than their own. Seeing the Western system of marriage institutionalized in foreign cultures as the Christian way of contracting marriage is pathetic. Christian missionaries working among the Igala people disregarded the Igala traditional form of contracting marriage and replaced it with their own form, which they regarded as being the Christian way. This foreign way often created marital problems and disaffection in families as traditional rites were rejected and Western answers sought for marital questions.

The church planter needs to be careful about his own receptor's tradition concerning the institution of marriage. He needs to study the way his receptors contract marriage so that he can establish biblical principles for the Christians he has led to Christ. He needs to understand the meaning, mode, and rules regulating marriage among his receptors. Meaningful biblical teaching ought to be established on a sound understanding of the features of traditional and contemporary marriage practice.

Furthermore, it is essential to recognize the perception of

separation, divorce and remarriage by the people. In applying scriptural principles to marital problems, the church planter should guard against using his own culture and understanding in relating to the issues that need to be addressed.

CONTEXTUAL MISSIOLOGICAL QUESTIONS

The cross-cultural church planter needs to ask questions that would help him see the distinction between what constitutes Christian marriage, his own system of contracting marriage and the system practiced by his receptors. To avoid the situation such as the one created by Western missionaries among the Igala Christians, church planters should be prepared to be flexible and allow traditional practices of their receptors to be subjected to Biblical principles. In doing so, he should ask questions which would provide a better foundation on which to establish his teachings.

Some have suggested that local believers should be trusted to formulate their own principles for Christian marriage. Such principles would draw upon the Bible and the tradition of the people. Church planters could play a vital role to guide and teach such principles. The following questions may provide both the church planter and his receptors with some issues to watch for.

(1) What is traditional marriage and how is it different from Biblical Christian marriage and Western Christian marriage? The church planter needs to ask himself what his own system is and evaluate it with the Bible.

(2) What are the essential elements of biblical Christian marriage that must be retained in a traditional Christian marriage? What other cultural elements must not be rctaincd and why must they be removed and rejected?

(3) What are the purposes of marriage in the culture of the missionary and of the receptors? Different cultures have different purposes and such purposes determine the success or failure of many marriages. For instance, in many West African societies, people marry for procreation in order to keep the lineage or family name. In some Western societies, some people marry with the agreement that there should be no children at all. In these two instances, children could

terminate or stabilize these marriages. The church planter needs to know why people marry. Expectations and understanding of such expectations can help him deal with marital problems.

(4) Why do people separate, divorce or marry more than one wife? On what basis must the church planter deal with these marital problems? The ability of the church planter to help people solve their problems rests on his knowledge of their culture (where they are coming from and what led to their decisions and actions), and the right application of the Scriptures. The usual temptation to impose one's convictions based on understanding his own culture must be avoided.

(5) What changes in regard to marriage are taking place and how do people react to them? What changes should the church planter introduce and how should he go about introducing them without causing conflict?

(6) What type of leaders are likely to be respected and effective, married or unmarried? What type of marriage is best for potential leaders or more likely to be accepted by most of the receptors?

(7) What elements in Western marriage, already accepted by the people as unscriptural, must be replaced with traditional form?

(8) How can I best help my receptors to see marriage as a symbol of Christ and His church?

CASE STUDY: IGALA MARRIAGE INSTITUTION

Among the Igala people, marriage is a crucial stage in a person's life cycle. There are different types of marriages in Igala society today. The most common types are traditional marriage, Christian marriage, contemporary Christian marriage, and Muslim marriage.

TRADITIONAL MARRIAGE

Marriage is referred to as *udama oko kpai oya*, "the joining of the male and female." There are at least three main purposes of marriage. These are listed in order of importance:

1) Procreation in order to keep the family or lineage name going
2) The need for a man to have somebody to cook for him

3) Enhancement of one's social status. Marriage brings responsibility and, in Igala society, one needs to have a family before he is said to be a responsible person.

Igala have no written rules governing marriage; however, most follow unwritten customary rules which may vary from clan to clan. Three main practices, found in all clans within the Igala society, are central for Igala traditional marriage.

1) Arrangements are negotiated by a go-between, *utogba oya*
2) The bride price is paid, *ome-oya*
3) Family backgrounds of bride and groom is seen as compatible, *ene-kone 'che.*

The go-between, usually a relative of the bridegroom or a family friend of either the bride or the groom, must satisfy the bride's parents with relevant background information on the bridegroom's family. The bride's parents are particularly interested in learning about the reputation of the groom's family, their ability to feed themselves, and whether or not they are hospitable. They are concerned about whether their attitude toward women is cruel or kind.

The groom's family seeks to discover whether there are cases of infertility/impotency, whether there are cases of diseases which are contagious and hereditary, and whether there are cases of immorality such as adultery or fornication. Both families are concerned about questionable character; whether there is a thief, lazy person, or other disreputable character in that family. For a period of time the families research the lineage of the prospective spouse.

The concept of bride wealth is not primarily for economic interests, although that cannot be completely ruled out. It is rather a practice built into the system to help the men to love and appreciate their wives. If the women are given to the men without charge, the women will be looked upon as useless and worthless people.

MARRIAGE RULES

The Igala people have a rigid tradition which defines who one can marry and who one cannot marry. Thus marriage is prohibited between:

1) A brother and his sister, *amomaye,* in the lineage and extended family.
2) Cross-cousins, including second and third generations, *amoma omaye,* MBD, FZD, etc.
3) A man and his niece, *one kpai oma omayewn*
4) A woman and her nephew, *one kpai oma omayewn*

Marriage is allowed between those who have no blood relationship and on cases such as:

1) Levirate, *oya ogwu*
2) Filial widow inheritance, *oya ata one* (this is very rare today.)
3) Fourth generation uterine kin, *ebita* and *oma onobule*

It should be emphasized that incest is forbidden, while marriage rules require that one must marry from outside his or her family, extended family and lineages. Marriage is allowed between lineages within the same clan if no known patrilineal links can be established.

MODE OF TRADITIONAL MARRIAGE

The mode of traditional marriage is as complex as the practice of marriage itself. There are at least seven major steps to be taken in the marriage process and all these must be within the contract period of seven years. The seven steps are:

Step 1: The groom's father goes to the bride's father to ask the latter to assist him in raising his boy. If the bride's father agrees, that sets the contract rolling and this period is called *alekago* which means "going to see" or "going to observe."

Step 2: The groom goes to visit the bride's father and stays for a period of three days. He returns to his own house to stay for five days. During this visit, the groom gives two shillings to his prospective bride through the girl's mother. It should be noted that there should be no direct contact between the bride and groom at all.

Step 3: After spending five days at his own house, the boy goes back to visit his would-be in-laws for seven days.

During this visit, he comes with five shillings for his bride and three balls of salt to be given to the mother-in-law through the go-between. After this, he returns to his own house for thirteen days. Processed salt is significant because it was brought by the white people and was a scarce commodity. Prior to this, people used natural salt dug from the ground.

Step 4: The boy goes back to visit his parents-in-law for two months with five balls of salt to be given to the mother-in-law through the go-between. At the end of two months, he returns to his own house to stay for one month. He gives seven shillings to his bride during this visit.

At this stage, should the boy become uninterested in the girl, he will stop any further contacts and inform the go-between immediately. Refunds will be made. This period, covering steps one through four, is called a period of observation, *alekago.*

Step 5: After spending one month at his own house, he goes back to his in-laws to stay indefinitely. This time, he will present seven balls of salt and one tin of palm oil. Note that the mother-in-law will keep all these things presented by the groom for as long as two years. It is only after the marriage proposal is well established, firm and grounded that she will make use of the presents.

Step 6: The sixth step comes during the period of tax paying. The groom obtains permission from his parents-in-law to proceed home to work to earn enough money for the payment of poll tax for himself and his bride. If consent is given, he leaves for three months.

Step 7: This is perhaps the most important aspect of the seven year period. As the girl reaches maturation (puberty), arrangements will be made for the marriage ritual called *Ebo-oji.* The go-between will be called to arrange for this ritual. The groom will be required to provide a he-goat, a hen, and a cock for the feast. At the end of the ritual, the mother-in-law will allow for the first-time physical and sexual contact, *oya edutunyi*, between the two. It should be realized that sexual contact is allowed only with permission of the mother-in-law.

The purpose of the marriage ritual, *ebo-oji*, is to ensure that spiritual forces that could hinder good health, fertility and child production are appeased. The *Ebo-oji* ritual is for both the groom and his bride. It is believed that without this ritual the act of marriage could result in the girl falling sick and the boy becoming impotent.

After the first sexual contact, the boy is expected to kneel and thank the mother-in-law in appreciation. At this time also, the mother-in-law will demand to know from the groom if her daughter was a virgin and whether he was able to discharge his own responsibility (reference to potency).

If the girl is determined to be a virgin by the husband (groom), he must pay five shillings in appreciation to the mother-in-law for raising her daughter well. Although the bride, from this point, is considered the legal wife of the groom, marriage has not been customarily consummated. The man must complete his bride price rites over the ensuing seven years. The husband remains under the authority of his in-laws and has no authority over his wife. He may talk to her only through his mother-in-law. There is no exception to this rule.

Finally, if after the *Ebo-oji* ritual the girl does not become pregnant, another ritual called *Ikpakachi* must be performed; in this, the groom provides a goat, cock, and a piece of white cloth to be offered to the spirits of fertility to enable the bride to conceive. When she becomes pregnant, another ritual, called *Amude-oma*, must be performed for the protection of the baby.

After a seven year period, the marriage rites are completed. The groom is free and can therefore choose where he wants to live and what he wants to do.

FEATURES OF TRADITIONAL MARRIAGE

After the seven year marriage process, the couple usually establishes residence patrilocally in the lineage of the groom's father. However, some people choose to live matrilocally for one of two reasons: either the groom's house or home is not in good order (because of some harmful spiritual problem), or the man needs to take care of his parents-in-law, especially where they do not have male children in the family. It is, however, at the discretion of the husband.

People have preference in choosing a mate. This is especially true of the men. They choose who they should marry and consider what qualities are needed. Women are rarely given the opportunity to choose. This practice is, however, changing today as some believe that lack of choice and preference has led to polygamy and divorce.

Igala prefer large families and strongly emphasize an extended family network. The desire to maintain a large family in the traditional system often leads to polygamy. The number of wives in Igala society is determined by the nature of each family. However, many people believe that the desire for children, preferred sex of children, and sexual desire have increased the frequency of polygamy.

Sex in traditional marriage is regarded as a sacred thing. Partners do not talk about it openly and children are normally kept out of any discussion involving sexual matters. Igala avoid physical contact between the husband and wife in public or before their children. Further, they do not sleep in the same room and may not have sex during the day.

The sanctity of sex, sex roles, the importance of fertility and male children and marriage rituals are issues for the church planter to reckon with. There should be biblical and practical teaching on these issues crucial to people like the Igala.

ISSUES AND PROBLEMS OF POLYGAMY

Polygamy is prominent among the Igala people. It is a practice where a man marries more than one wife legally. Although it is prominent and is widely practiced, the Igala do not all agree that it is needful.

There are many reasons why men practice polygamy. Some men take many wives because they want to be respected; managing a family with many wives signifies that the man is wealthy. It is also practiced because of the intensive sexual desire of the men, and especially those whose wives are breast-feeding. It is a taboo for a man to have sexual relations with a woman who is breast-feeding. It is believed that the child will die if such sexual relations are maintained.

There are many advantages to polygamy. Because most Igala people are farmers, the need for labor is crucial. Men marry many wives because of the labor provided by the wives, and their male children imitate this behavior. Polygamy helps the man to put his wives under control as the wives will be busy competing among themselves. With many wives, the men have somebody to take care of their children when one of the wives dies, and they will not have to search for wives afresh. Other advantages include a desire for many children and fulfillment of sexual desire within marriage while his wife or wives may be breastfeeding.

Polygamy has its disadvantages. It causes the wives to compete for their husband's attention thereby impeding the family unity. The competitive spirit of their wives is often reflected in the children showing little affection for one another; the net result is a lack of family unity. The father in a polygamous family which produces many children may be too busy and not have sufficient time to invest in raising the children well. Satisfying the sexual desire of many wives takes a lot of physical energy which may affect a man's health. Furthermore, the inability of the man to meet the sexual needs of his wives may cause them to develop interest in other men. Looking outside the marriage for satisfaction demoralizes the whole family, endangers the husband, whose life may be threatened by competing men and exposes the family to the hazards of infectious diseases caused by promiscuity.

CONTEMPORARY IGALA MARRIAGE

There have been a number of changes in the Igala traditional marriage system. These changes, which came mainly as a result of the contacts Igala had with other people, could also be attributed to other factors. Some of these are:

1) Non-traditional religions (Islam and Christianity)
2) Modernity (education and urbanization)
3) Economic issues
4) Nature of human culture (changefulness) and desire to imitate.

With the influence and pressure of these factors, the nature of Igala traditional marriage has been greatly altered. At present, there are three ways by which marriages are contracted in the contemporary Igala society. These three ways are the methods of the three main religious groups of the Igala: traditional religion, Christianity, and Islam.

CONTEMPORARY TRADITIONAL MARRIAGE

The present day Igala marriage is totally different than the traditional. In contemporary marriage, there are three essential features: courtship, engagement and consummation of marriage.

First is the dating/courtship period. As with traditional marriage, a go-between is appointed, this time by the groom's parents, to negotiate with the bride's family. Dating and courtship is a time in which potential problems that are likely to arise from either the boy or the girl might be resolved. During the second period, the appointed go-between arranges for the engagement ceremony after the girl's family gives their consent. The third and final step comes after the bride price is paid at the engagement ceremony. This period is when all necessary rituals such as *Ebo-oji* and *Ikpakachi* are performed. Once the rituals are performed satisfactorily, the bride is ready to join her husband.

The process is short, swift, and less complicated. It is, however, conditioned by one important thing. When some would-be in-laws see that their would-be son-in-law is wealthy, some traditional formalities are waived. Money solves the problems that may hinder the progress of the present day marriage process.

CONTEMPORARY CHRISTIAN MARRIAGE

Before the introduction of Christian marriage, Igala Christians were subjected to the traditional method of marrying. However, the introduction of Christianity was followed by a new system of marriage. This new system brought untold hardship on the early Igala Christians who had no converts to marry. With time, the evangelistic activities of missionaries yielded fruit and many Igala people became Christians and so could find life partners.

Christian marriage at the initial stage was similar to the traditional method with a few exceptions. The exceptions were centered around the issue of the bride price introduced into Christian marriage against the traditional method of bride service. Others had to do with fertility rituals such as *Ebo-oji* or *Ikpakachi*, which the Christians found unscriptural and protested.

As time went on, Christian marriage led to the introduction or acceptance of dating and courtship. Arranged marriages were no longer acceptable as the "will of God" replaced the "will of the parents." As people began to decide for themselves, they had the opportunity to get together to know one another better. Western education also influenced the rejection of arranged marriages.

Another change involves the practice of engagement at which period dowries are paid. Contemporary Christian marriage has made this ceremony a big issue where much money is spent on feasting. The former practice involved only a plate of cola-nuts and the payment of the agreed bride price. And whereas engagement was formerly followed by a wedding ceremony, engagement is now prolonged until the groom recuperates from the engagement expenses.

When the engagement is not broken, it ends in a formal wedding in the church. Where the couple is found to be involved in sexual intercourse during engagement, pregnancy cancels their dream for a church wedding, because the church does not wed those found to have engaged in premarital sexual relations.

It is important to point out that where a church wedding is performed, the entire program and activities, dresses and addresses are a replica of Western weddings. And in spite of the anti-Western attitude and spirit in most church teachings and practices, most young people will prefer to go into debt just to make sure the formalities of Western Christian weddings are performed. This is an area where Western ways have never been challenged even though the wedding formalities have no direct relation to Igala culture.

IGALA MUSLIM MARRIAGE

The Muslim marriage has also taken the same course Christian marriage has taken, with only a few distinctions. The concept of courtship (which is new) is accepted by most people. Many families tolerate it because they have no absolute control over their sons or daughters.

Similarly, while parental consent is always a key factor, many will go ahead and marry even without the consent of their parents. The issue of complete autonomy for the girls is still an illusion. In Igala society, Muslim parents still have a great deal of control over who their daughters marry.

In Muslim marriage, engagement involving the payment of dowries is practiced and this is followed by a wedding ceremony. There are two types of wedding ceremonies and the basic difference is in the scope. While *Awele* is small, *Iyawo* is a big ceremony. Another difference is that *Iyawo* is only for the first time brides. Those who are remarrying and small scale first time weddings will be *Awele.*

ANALYSIS OF CONTEMPORARY MARRIAGE PRACTICES

These three contemporary marriage practices discussed have replaced the original traditional system. The church planter needs to realize changing dynamics among his receptors so that teachings relate to real issues people face and live with.

EDARU-OKO NWOYA, "DIVORCE"

When a marriage fails and the partners split up, it is referred to as *"edaru-oko nwoya,"* divorce. When the husband initiates the divorce proceedings, he is said to have left or rejected his wife, *Ekoya,* and if the wife leaves or rejects her husband, that act is called *ekoko.* Separation, *Edaru,* does occur at the preliminary, *ababa,* stages of marital problems. The wife may decide to leave her husband temporarily or the husband may decide to send his wife away to her family. In matters of divorce, in addition to sending the wife from her matrimonial home, the husband may claim the bride price paid and all personal belongings of the wife which he bought for her. This is, however, optional. Individual husbands decide what is best for them.

CAUSES OF SEPARATION AND DIVORCE

The husband may separate or divorce his wife, *oko ekoya,* on the following grounds or reasons:

1. If the wife is barren, *agaji.*
2. If the wife bears only female children, *oma onobule.*
3. If the wife is suspected of being a witch, *ochu.*
4. If the wife has bad conduct or is adulterous, *abi biene/oko eje.*
5. If the wife does not know how to cook or take care of her domestic work, *obo.*
6. If the wife does not respect and honor her husband and the husband's family members, *imo jima onen.*
7. If she is not sexually responsive, *ije boko dachin.*
8. If she opposes her husband's desire to marry additional wives, *itene obugwun.*
9. If she quarrels or fights with her partners (her husband's wives or concubines, *ogwu-eja).*
10. If the husband's family does not like her.
11. If the wife becomes ill and the husband does not like to continue to care for her.

The wife may initiate divorce or separation, *oya ekoko,* proceedings for the following reasons:

1. If the husband cannot provide for her, *oko wn dujewn nun.*
2. If the husband refuses to have sex with her, *oko kobodachi.*
3. If the husband has become impotent, *akpino.*
4. If the husband is wicked, *alibiene.*
5. If the husband's family hates her, *amomaye okown achulaka.*
6. If the husband wants to marry more wives.
7. If the husband will not marry another wife to help her.
8. If she finds another man that she prefers, *onekele omune.*
9. If she cannot conceive, *inye fun.*
10. If her children continue to die at birth, *abikwu.*
11. If the husband is sick or facing a serious physical handicap.

It should be realized the wife, though married, is still close to her own family, and her husband is also close to his own family. Both of them listen to advice from their respective families. The advice they get could either lead them into separation or save their marriage. Pressure from extended family members of both parties should never be undermined.

The issue of interest and power can be clearly seen in the matter of separation or divorce. The husband has interests he needs to protect. As long as his interests are not met by his wife, his powers are challenged and threatened, and he will be looked down upon by the society as a weak man.

Similarly, the wife has her own interests and although she does not have ultimate power, she will pull strings as soon as she sees the weak points of her husband. This can be seen in cases where the husband has physical problems (deformity, impotency, handicaps, poverty). She will make sure her interests are served if she finds such areas for power negotiation.

Separation and divorce is common and devastating. It is especially true if children are brought into the relationship. Because it is a problem that cannot be legislated against, church planters should see that discipleship and teaching on marriage issues are well organized to prevent and heal problems. To wait until a marriage relationship crumbles to offer biblical counsel is like keeping a life vest from a drowning person.

EDABINOKO ABE KOYA, "REMARRIAGE"

Remarriage, *edabi noko abe koya,* occurs frequently. There are two basic types of remarriages in Igala society: between a man who is remarrying a woman he has divorced; or between divorced persons or widows, *oya-ukuoko,* and widowers, *ene koya wn lekwu.*

The concept of remarriage should be distinguished from Igala filial widow inheritance, *oya-ata wn,* and the levirate system, *oya-ogwu.* The filial widow inheritance and levirate marriage are not considered remarriages since these marriages are within the same family.

HOW PEOPLE PERCEIVE REMARRIAGE

Although this has become a frequent practice, it is not usually looked upon as honorable. This is especially true when a woman involved in a remarriage is divorced on grounds of adultery and bad conduct. However, if she divorced on the ground of the husband's wicked attitude or inability to provide for her, she will stand a better chance of enjoying her new marriage relationship.

In the same way, men who constantly divorce and remarry are

not looked at as responsible people. Even where they may have genuine cases, the fact that they have gone through many marriages discredits their characters.

The story is different for widows and widowers. They are looked upon with sympathy and are so treated. In some cases, however, some widows are looked upon with suspicion and ignominy if they are suspected to be either witches or at fault in their husband's death.

It should be pointed out too that second marriages, *oyaonukeji* and *okoenukeji*, are looked at generally as second-class marriages. Although remarriages are accepted in the society, women who have many cases of divorce are looked upon either as trouble-makers or promiscuous, *ajoko*. They may have to live with this insult and degradation all their lives.

APPLICATION: IMPLICATIONS FOR CHURCH PLANTING

Four main issues of marriage are significant and should be addressed by the church planter. These issues are the importance of children, polygamy, divorce and remarriage, and changing tradition.

One of the purposes of marriage is procreation in order to keep the lineage or family name going. In fact, male children are preferred over female children for the sake of perpetuating the family name. This explains the desire to marry one who can bear children. It also explains why the Igala perform rituals for fertility. The church needs to know the pressure young couples go through in their quest for children. Divorce and remarriage is not allowed for any reason by the Igala church. While this is not an attempt to reject such sanctions, the church needs to come to grips with the pressure people face and learn to deal with those problems, especially since childlessness often results in divorce or polygamy.

Polygamy is an issue the church has had to deal with since the coming of Christianity to the Igala people. It is also an issue which the church must look at objectively, studying its causes and circumstances so that polygamous problems can be dealt with scripturally and sympathetically. The church needs to objectively analyze polygamous cases with the ultimate desire to help people and show them how to help themselves.

Marital problems often lead to separation and, consequently, divorce. The responsibility of the church to married couples should not stop on their wedding day. The church should see the need to introduce a counseling and teaching program for married couples aimed at healing marital problems.

The church must also study each case of divorce carefully in dealing with the matter of remarriages. Furthermore, the church should recognize the impact of separation, divorce and remarriage, their effects on children and make provision to minister to them as well.

The church needs to be alerted to changes taking place in marriages today. Contemporary marriage practice in Igala society needs to be scrutinized with the Bible, and the church has a responsibility to see that changes are scriptural and healthy to the institution of marriage in the society.

Chapter Five

POLITICAL AND SOCIAL STRUCTURE

In any culture, political leadership and social structures exist. What is unique is how these structures differ from culture to culture. The church planter will find that his own system of political leadership and social structures are different from those of his receptors. Although there may be some similarities in motive and objectives for assuming leadership roles, the church planter needs to know the system existing in his receptor's culture and to understand and respect these institutions.

Furthermore, the church planter should identify with the indigenous forms of leadership, social activities and hierarchies in his teachings as well as in his organization of the local congregation. This type of identification would go a long way to stabilize his teachings, as people can easily relate to their own traditional forms instead of being coerced to a foreign structure.

Introducing an indigenous method of leadership does not imply that culture would replace the Bible. The church planter should not baptize his own system in the Bible and impose it on his receptors. The Bible should be the yardstick for measuring the use of traditional forms and their introduction into leadership and social structures in the church. Nevertheless, the church planter needs to understand the political and social structures of the people he works with in order to be effective among them. He could gain such understanding by identifying with his receptors and asking them about what he sees, observes, hears and reads about them.

CONTEXTUAL MISSIOLOGICAL QUESTIONS

Every church planter faces social context issues in ministry regardless of where he ministers. In spite of differences on issues due to differences in culture, geographical location and ethnicity, several general missiological questions would guide the church planter in dealing with social context questions of their receptors. This is also true of the political and social structures. The following questions may be used by the church planter in his determination to relate more to the issues involved in politics and the society and how they affect the church and individual believers in the church.

i. In relation to leadership, there is a need to ask how leaders are traditionally recruited or appointed. What qualities do the people seek in their leaders? How do they get their authority? What is the selection process? Is the leadership democratic? To whom is the leadership responsible? How independent of external influence is the leadership?
ii. In relation to decision-making, who is responsible for decision-making? How are decisions made? How is power exercised? How effective are the leaders in delegating?
iii. In relation to support, how do leaders get support? What form of support is often enlisted?

These questions would help the church planter to find out how the leadership works in terms of its structure, use of power, authority, legitimacy, support and decision-making; and how these can be adopted by the church.

iv. What is the social hierarchy of this culture and how will the structure affect the organization of the church in relation to its leadership, interpersonal relationships, and corporate outreach programs? What role does economic power play in determining one's social status and how does the church planter fit into the social hierarchy of his receptors? What is the impact of age and gender on social relations? How can the rich and poor in separate social hierarchies unite in the church? What role should the church planter play in bringing about an egalitarian atmosphere in the church and should he?

v. What social events and activities are the receptors involved in and how can the gospel be preached through this structure? What should the relationship of the Christian and non-Christian be in relation to social events and activities in which both may be participants? To what extent is economic interest a major determining factor in social events and activities and how can the church become a major factor? How far can the church planter involve himself in social events and activities?

vi. In connection with traditional music and dance, how should the church planter encourage the introduction of traditional form? What should be the basis for the church planter's examination of the relevance of traditional musical instruments to be used in church worship, his own culture, his receptor's, the Bible or all? What needs are served in the use of traditional forms of worship and what significant contribution can be made to church planting?

CASE STUDY: IGALA VILLAGE POLITICAL LEADERSHIP

DESCRIPTION OF OFUGO VILLAGE

Ofugo village is situated in the Dekina Local Government Area of Benue State. Dekina Local Government Area is one of the four divisions into which the former Igala kingdom has been split. The other three divisions of local government areas are Idah, Ankpa and Bassa (see Figure 5).

Ofugo village lies between Dekina town to the east and Ayangba town to the north. The distance between Lokoja (Niger-Benue Confluence) and Ofugo is about fifty miles. It is one of the Odu Greater Area villages which constitute about one fourth of the Dekina Local Government Area.

A small village with about one thousand people, it has three clans and four wards. The three clans are the Ibieju, Onoja and Iko. Each of these clans has a *madaki*, "chief," and an *ogijo olopu*, "clan head." The ward chiefs perform administrative roles, while the ward heads

Figure 5 MAP OF IGALA AREA SHOWING THE DISTRICTS

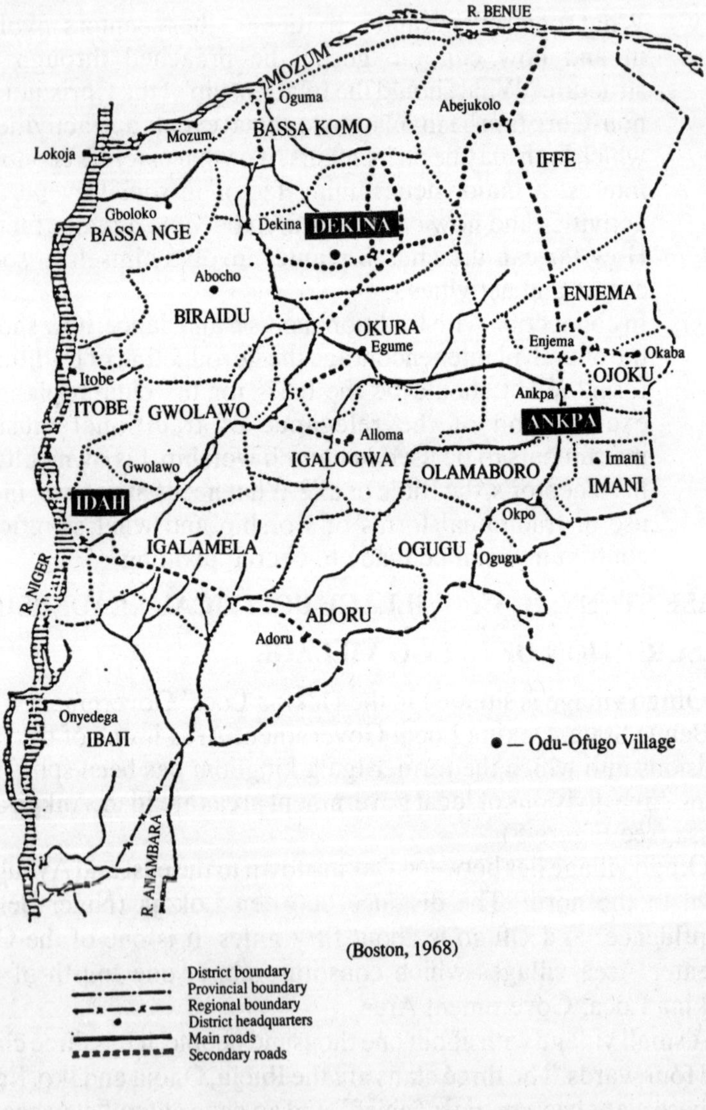

(Boston, 1968)

are responsible for customary matters. The village chiefs are nominated by their clan members and are appointed by the government while clan head is a position held by the oldest member of a clan.

The four wards represent the three clans, and the immigrant residents. The original settlers regard the new residents as clanless people because they have no title to land within the village. The new residents are also zoned, each to one of the three ward chiefs.

There are many lineages in each ward. It is difficult to be exact, as most clan ancestors have had many children through polygamous marriages. At least, four lineages are found in each clan.

Ofugo village has a number of meeting points which are centers of social activities. These include the shrine, mosque, church, market place, stream, elementary school, and health clinic. These meeting points are well scattered throughout the village. However, the market place which is also the location for all village meetings, is centrally located between the three clans representing the original settlers.

This structure of Ofugo is typical of Igala villages. The Igala people congregate on clan, lineage and family lines, while those in the immigrant category tend to live in a new settlement area allocated to them by the original settlers. Usually, these settlement areas are outside the clan's bounded residential area.

Four reasons are given for immigration to Ofugo village. A traditional reason is that of intra-tribal war; contemporary reasons are relative to quests for fertile farmland, a source of water and the extinction of one's village, due to mysterious and frequent deaths.

There are many points of similarities with other villages. Apart from the living patterns, the location of important meeting places are well scattered, while the village market is always centrally located. It is also important to stress that each village has a ward chief and clan head.

Most Igala people live in rural settings. Only three towns, each with a population between twenty- and forty-thousand people, may be considered to be semi-urban (Ankpa, Dekina and Idah). There is pipe borne water supply and electricity to Ankpa, Idah and Dekina towns.

Running water and electricity are perhaps two of the three

distinctions that can be made between a typical Igala village and town; the third is population size.

THE VILLAGE CHIEFS

The British colonial government in Nigeria introduced a system of indirect rule which reduced the influence and power of Attah the Igala king. As the Igala Kingdom was divided into districts, district heads were appointed by the Attah. The Attah also retained his own traditional rulers who were in charge of groups of villages or clans. Administrative power was in the hands of the district heads, Gagos and Madakis. The system of indirect rule was used by the colonial administration so that the King and chiefs, who knew their own people very well, could help the colonial administration achieve their aims and objectives. Where there was no centralized leadership, the colonial administration imposed a direct rule.

At the village level, Madakis, "ward chiefs," were appointed to lead each clan or ward. The number of Madakis to a village depends on how large and densely populated a village is. In some densely populated villages, a Gago, "village chief," was appointed to lead the Madakis. To assist the Madakis to pass on information to their constituencies, Achokolobias, "messengers," were appointed. These three political statuses governed the administration of their village. Their appointment and authority can be summarized as follows:

1. *Gago:* "village chief" was appointed by the *Atta* Igala and was usually a beaded chief. He had authority for a large village or a group of small villages.
2. *Madaki:* "ward chief" was appointed by the colonial district head to represent the clan or ward from which he came. He had authority and responsibility to assist the *Gago* in the collection of taxes and other dues.
3. *Achokolobia:* "messenger" was appointed by the colonial district head on the advice of the village chief to help each ward chief disseminate information to the villagers.

It must be mentioned that the powers of these village leaders have been greatly limited by the present system of government which gives ultimate supervisory authority to the local elected governments.

THE VILLAGE COUNCIL

Until recently, the chiefs were the sole authority in the village. Their powers and authority was not challenged since they were employees of the Igala native authority under colonial rule. Since Independence, village councils were constituted to assist the chiefs in the running of the affairs of their domain. The present local government is more democratic than the former Igala native authority which was centralized with wider powers and control.

The village Council or village Central Committee, as they are known, has many members, mainly leaders from each ward. On the advice and nomination of the members of each ward, the ward chief appoints two or three persons to represent it.

The need for development and government presence led the people to revolt against the traditional method whereby the village chief or ward chief speaks for their various communities. With the formation of the Councils or Committees, the chiefs are mandated to address specific community needs instead of his own wants. They assist the chiefs in the decision-making process. Some of the specific roles of these Committees or Councils are:

1) To organize community development projects.
2) To mobilize the community for self-improvement projects.
3) To organize vigilante groups to watch the activities of the men of the underworld.
4) To help the chiefs to collect levies and enforce certain by-laws.
5) To encourage socialization and ensure that people do not wander about without responsibilities. Such idle people are punished because idleness may lead them into evil practices in the village. It is the responsibility of every bona-fide resident to see to it that order, discipline and security are maintained.

People appointed to serve on the Committee are not paid. They enjoy being there because of their desire to help the village develop. Such developments are for the good of everyone. It is also seen as a responsible and prestigious position because of the advantage of being associated with good projects in the village. Since they are appointed by the ward chief on the recommendation of their wards, dissolution is left in the hands of the villagers.

While appointed members are male adults, women are normally represented by a member who is perhaps a leader in the women's meeting. The young people are also allowed to take part by sending a representative to the Committee or Council meetings.

The Council or Committee has the power to plan and execute projects on behalf of the villagers. This must be done, however, in consultation with the village chiefs. The village chiefs also must consult the Committee or Council on important matters and decisions must be by consensus. Majority vote is seldom exercised.

The final authority to remove either the Committee members or the village chiefs depends on the villagers. They have the final say and decisions on such cases are reached from each ward or clan. This new process has curtailed the excesses of the village chiefs who in times past were the supreme authorities in their respective domains.

People look for many good qualities in a person they wish to appoint as their leader. There is a special emphasis on conduct and character, reliability and trustworthiness. Another quality sought is "sociableness" or how the leader gets along with people and whether or not he is outspoken or timid. In addition to these, three important issues or questions are usually raised:

a) Is he a son of the soil? Where are his parents from? What is their background? Were they free men or slaves?
b) Is he married? Is he a responsible husband and father or does he run here and there? Is he stable? What type of friends does he keep?
c) Does he have a house in his father's compound? Is he committed to his own family? To his village? If not, he will be looked down upon.

Although people occasionally use money to influence political appointments, it is unlikely that money would give credibility to one whose personal character was questionable or objectionable. These qualities are crucial when appointments to positions of authority are being considered.

Once a leader is appointed, further support depends on his

effectiveness as a leader and how much he is able to do and bring into his village. A commitment to one's constituency and to the needs of his people are the main sources of his support.

The church planter needs to understand the dynamics of village political leadership, to be sensitive to the various cultural issues involved in the selection of a leader and his subsequent responsibilities. Since the church is planted within the same socio-cultural context, every attempt should be made to relate to the patterns existing there.

Cases: Decision-making process

Decision-making processes among the Igala vary even on critical issues. The nature of the process depends on the nature of the business at hand. The following are examples of decision-making processes at the clan and village levels at Ofugo village. (For the sketch of Ofugo village showing what a typical village looks like see Figure 6).

Case #1: **Decision-Making at the Clan Level**

In 1985, there was a land dispute at Ofugo between Owunu-tubioko clan and another clan not indigenous to Ofugo. The clan head (the eldest male member of the clan) called all the family elders together to discuss how the dispute could be resolved. The family elders brought their male children so that they could listen to the proverbs and stories which the elders told as they tried to map out strategies. This time, the elders reviewed the oral tradition of how they had come to settle and own the disputed land. The elders agreed unanimously that it was necessary to take the case to court for adjudication. Before taking the matter to court, they had to agree among themselves:

— That the case was viable
— That the male children of the families should be consulted and be made to contribute towards this case
— That those in the family who were not in support of this case be ostracized or be denied their share or inheritance

The meeting was called or arranged by the clan elders. The various families and lineages in the clan were represented by their

Figure 6

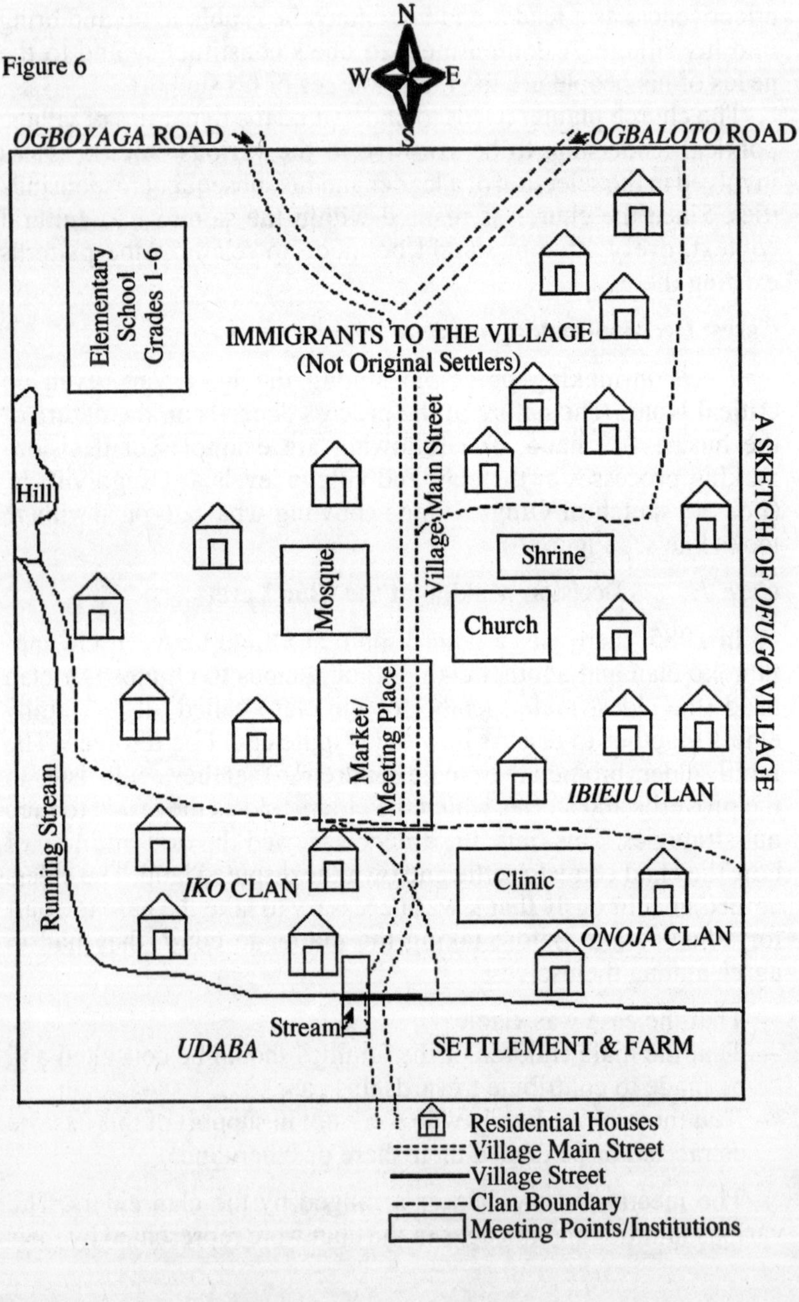
N
W
E
S
OGBOYAGA ROAD
OGBALOTO ROAD
Elementary School Grades 1-6
IMMIGRANTS TO THE VILLAGE
(Not Original Settlers)
Hill
Village Main Street
Shrine
Mosque
Church
Market/ Meeting Place
IBIEJU CLAN
Running Stream
IKO CLAN
Clinic
ONOJA CLAN
Stream
UDABA
SETTLEMENT & FARM
A SKETCH OF *OFUGO* VILLAGE
Residential Houses
Village Main Street
Village Street
Clan Boundary
Meeting Points/Institutions

elders and male children. The eldest member in the clan presided over the clan meeting and made sure that the decision was unanimous.

Adult members who refused to support the meeting with their presence were declared enemies of the clan. Their right to inheritance in the clan was restricted.

Male children were allowed to attend as observers and were made to listen to oral histories and tradition concerning the land under dispute for the purpose of learning. However, some children from a higher socio-economic class were allowed to speak and participate in the decision-making process.

This method of decision-making was based on family and lineage representations. The criteria for selecting representatives were sex and age. Another criterion followed in determining who should speak and participate was socio-economic status. But, regardless of the will of individuals and strong influence from some prominent members of the clan, a unanimous decision was reached, and dissenters were punished for their unbecoming behavior.

Case #2: **Decision-making at the Village Level**

Setting: General meeting of the village

Present: The Villagers
The Executive Committee members
The Madaki's and their representatives
The working class representatives

Presiding: The Executive Committee chairman

Issue:

The issue to be discussed was the construction of the main Ofugo village street beginning from Ate-Ofagwu Junction through Udaba, about two kilometers. Other projects associated with this were the construction of a staff quarters for the Health Center staff and a bridge over Ajego stream to facilitate easy transportation services.

Procedure:

1) Opening prayer with everyone standing.
2) The reading of the minutes of the previous general meeting: The assistant secretary read the minutes of the last general meeting

and requested members to approve them. One member so moved and his motion was seconded by two other men. The Chairman was then asked to sign the approved minutes. This process was so unfamiliar to the people that they waited for the secretary to go through the formalities.

Matters arising:

The Secretary explained to those present the reason for the meeting and the need for members to organize and conduct themselves wisely as the meeting progressed. He then requested the Chairman to take full charge of the meeting.

The Chairman greeted members present and voiced his disappointment at the low attendance and the conspicuous absence of women. Having finished his own admonitory statements, he called on the Secretary to brief the villagers on the permit obtained from the state government for the imposition of levies for the community projects. Members were happy that the government had given formal approval, without which levies could not be imposed and collected.

Project description:

The projects before the Ofugo Community were three:

1) The construction of the main street including the dredging of the stream.
2) The construction of staff quarters for the Ofugo Community Health Clinic.
3) The construction of a bridge over the Ajego stream.

Villagers were asked to prioritize the projects. A unanimous decision was made to begin street construction. The project was important because rains had washed dirt, sand and debris from the street into the stream, the only source of water for the villagers.

The construction of the street would necessitate the construction of gutters and culverts to divert the water flowing into the stream. If the stream were dredged, more clean and drinkable water would be available.

Imposition of the levy:

In imposing the levy on the villagers and community residents at home and abroad, it was decided that three categories be created.

1) Male Adults (of marriageable age)
2) Females (of marriageable age)
3) Working class people (at home and abroad)

After debating how much should be paid by each category, it was finally decided that:

1) The men should pay N40
2) The women should pay N10
3) The working class should pay according to income. A minimum of N60 was set.

The decision to determine the amount to be paid by these categories was done by majority vote. It was difficult to reach a consensus because of the varied economic status and background of most members. However, everyone seemed to be satisfied by the imposition.

ANALYSIS OF CASES

These two cases differed significantly in who was invited to attend, who was given the right to speak, and how the decision was reached. The first case was one in which family or clan interest was an issue. The purpose was to reclaim a piece of disputed land. The second case had to do with the development of the village and concerned everybody. Therefore, it can be seen that the purpose of a meeting determined who should attend it.

In the first case, only elders of the clan and family elders were invited with their male children. Women and non-clan members were not invited. The second case involved all members regardless of age and gender.

The second meeting was formally organized. A chairman presided and a secretary kept a record of the proceedings. Village chiefs, committee members and some representatives of the local government were invited. The agenda was formal and systematic. The procedure was democratic and egalitarian. Everyone had the opportunity to speak. In the first case, the eldest man in the clan was in charge. Others were allowed to speak based on age and family. Young people were permitted to ask questions but could not readily express an opinion. No outsiders were permitted to attend. There was no program, no written agenda, and no minutes of the proceedings.

In the first case, the decision was unanimous and was reached by a consensus while in the second case it was based on a majority vote. The process for reaching the decision was lengthy and time consuming in the second case. In the first case, it was short and timely.

These two cases show how people change from one extreme to another. In the first meeting we have a traditional decision-making situation while in the second case, we have a modern form of decision-making. The basic reason for this difference is the nature and purpose of the meetings. As long as people's needs are being met, no one complains about social changes. In both cases a decision was reached with which the people were satisfied. The chairman of the second meeting was also involved in the first. He was willing to make changes and adjust for the sake of his own interests. The type of change can be witnessed today in Igala society.

It is important that the church planter be not only sensitive to the existing traditional structures, but that he become sensitive and open to changes in that society. People should not be forced to conform to any standard. Even when biblical standards are being violated, exercising restraint may prevent forcing people into legalism. Rebuking, exhorting, and admonishing in love are appropriate Christian responses, not the formulation of rules, regulations or codes of conduct in the church.

CASE STUDY: IGALA SOCIAL HIERARCHY

Igala divide the world of social relations into two categories, *abogijo,* "patron," and *oma-efowo,* "clients." This classification is based on socio-economic status in the Igala society.

In Igala concept, the idea of a middle group is not considered at all. The above classification gives no consideration to gender or age. At the village level where most people are poor, various terms are used to describe socio-economic positions. The following are the Igala identities which structure social hierarchy:

Patron identities, *abogijo*	Client identities, *oma-efowo*
Enelile, big person	*Enekekele,* small person
Anana, rich person	*Anale,* empty-handed person
Anoko, wealthy person	*Enobata,* poor person
Enojima, respectable person	*Ogwuchekwo,* ordinary person

The relationship between the patron and client is that of service. The clients often seek to serve or help the patrons with the aim of obtaining a reward or gift in return. Patrons offer prospective clients money and position, or influence and power.

Enelile, "big men," are usually political and government functionaries or educated and highly placed officials, whereas the wealthy businessmen are usually successful businessmen. These categories of people are many in the towns or cities and are not as influential and powerful.

Some Igala are neither very rich nor very poor; others are respected and have successful businesses but could not be considered wealthy people. Igala have no term to describe these types of people who are an emerging middle group. This social cadre includes school teachers, intermediate civil servants, self-employed persons and businessmen, village chiefs, and local politicians. People having these identities are in a position of ambiguity and conflict; the poorer segment of society view them as patrons, while the patron elite see them as inferior prospective clients. These "middle" people express great frustration at the demands of the client sector, which are based upon assumptions of wealth that they cannot sustain.

SYMBOLS OF IDENTITY

To determine what identity a person holds, cues are taken from certain practices, behaviors and life-styles. Some of these are:

1. The quality of food that one eats, *ola ujewn kiaje*
2. The quality of clothes that one wears, *ukpo kialo*
3. The number of people in one's household, *lkonown*
4. The type of house one owns, *ola unyi kine*
5. The properties one owns, *ewn ane kine*
6. The type of friends one keeps, *amonuku kine*
7. The manner and nature of one's utterances, *ola aluwn*

8. How one relates to people, *udagown ugbo amone*
9. One's involvement in social activities, *ichola wn efoja*
10. The geographical location of one's residence, *ugbo kidodo*

In Igala society, expectations and obligations depend on social status and position. The patron sector is expected to help those of the client sector. The type of help often provided is inadequate to make any significant difference. The poor are often kept under subjection to the rich.

In receiving help from the rich, the poor always remember an Igala proverb which says, *"Alu fewn je, anyo feju mu,"* "if the mouth has eaten something, the face or eyes become shy." No one wants to be bought or controlled through charity. The poor prefer to suffer rather than become slaves of the rich.

CASE STUDY: IGALA SOCIAL EVENTS AND ACTIVITIES

VOLUNTARY ASSOCIATIONS

Village social activities and events, in which the Igala interact with people other than kin and clan, widen their social sphere. Their social relationships are based on individual and corporate interests in the areas of economic, political, social, religious and cultural matters and are built around gender and age stratifications.

There are at least four forms of voluntary association in which people interact outside of their lineage and clan affiliation. These social activities serve specific purposes and interests. The participants in each activity are also well defined.

These associations which promote interpersonal relationships are significant in that they serve economic and political needs. For instance, several activities are socially beneficial to children and women since age and gender differentiations have limited their public role in the society. In these public meetings, the poor and lower class also tend to have fun and some of their psychological and emotional needs are met.

Oja

Oja is a voluntary society or club which is open to both sexes. Although young people may belong, they usually form their own *Oja* club in which their interests are served. The main purpose of the society is to serve as a financial institution for members. Usually members contribute a fixed amount either weekly, fortnightly or monthly to the society, thus saving their money to meet future obligations in the absence of banking services. They may then apply for needed loans and get help from society members in times of emergencies.

Meetings are held on each day contributions are due at which members socialize. The societies set a code of conduct for members. Questionable characters are disciplined. Thus, they also try to help their community shape behavior.

Ajuma

Ajuma is another voluntary society for adults of both sexes which functions like *Oja*. In addition, this society provides assistance to bereaved members and to those involved in social festivals and ceremonies. The economic interest served is the same as in the *Oja* society. Meetings are held on Friday of each week. Socialization includes the drinking of alcoholic beverages. Although *Ajuma* is for both men and women, they meet separately.

Owe and *Adakpo*

Owe is the mature men's organization, and *adakpo* is the young men's organization.

These are agricultural cooperative societies or clubs. Members come together collectively to provide labor needed on the farm on a rotational basis. The economic interests served in this society are great. More farm acreage leads to more production which, in turn, yields more crops. As more men get together to pool human resources, they not only serve economic needs, but also psychological and physiological needs.

Abolojo and *Amabakpa*

Abolojo (for Christians) and *Amabakpa* (for Muslims) are voluntary religious associations. Each conducts a number of religious, social, and economic activities in which members are involved and through which their spiritual, material, economic, and physical needs are met. These organizations are open to all sexes and ages. While the Christians meet in their churches on Sundays and every morning for worship and devotion, the Muslims meet on Fridays and every morning and evening for worship and prayers.

Studying how people socialize is important because it helps to determine the sphere of influence patterns. Some missionaries teach that Christians must not have anything to do with pagans or Muslims. They teach that Christians must be separated from unbelievers. Such lines of separation are heavily drawn on many mission fields.

Christians must be separated from the world, worldliness and even unbelievers; however, the Bible is not necessarily calling for physical separation. The Bible shows the need for Christians to maintain a unique lifestyle which is totally separate from the standard of the world; it is not a call for Christians to isolate themselves from the rest of the world.

For example, among the Igala people it is common to find Igala Christians with unbelieving relatives who are either pagans or Muslims. How can they possibly refuse to socialize with these relatives? What Christian testimony would that communicate? How can these Christians witness to their relatives if they cannot relate to them? The church planter needs to be careful in his teaching on biblical separation. People cannot be isolated for spirituality. The Bible says that believers are not of the world, but are in the world and have been left in the world as witnesses. Nevertheless, where social activities lead to immorality, idolatry, and dishonor to Christ and His Church, the Christians have no right to be present. This delicate balance ought to be maintained.

CASE STUDY: IGALA TRADITIONAL MUSIC AND DANCE

Music and dance are associated with the Igala social and religious festivals. They form an important aspect of village life. As in most Igala practices, music and dance vary with the participants and the functions. It is important to point out too that while most of the music and dances are indigenous, some have been brought in by other tribes or borrowed by Igala people.

Most Igala songs and dances have certain characteristics. They communicate diverse messages. Some of the characteristics are:

1) The music is fast and high-pitched
2) The dances require full concentration as they may involve

rotating in a circle or acrobatic displays

3) Some of the dances and songs communicate promiscuous messages
4) The dances are both individualistic and group
5) Individual singers and dancers are interested in attracting donations
6) Songs are directed at individuals and either sing their praises or rain insults on them
7) Some songs are directed at social issues of which people need to be aware.

At least fifteen different types of music and dances may be classified into three functional divisions (see Table 4). Eight of these are for social occasions. Both men and women of all ages are involved in most of these dances. The instruments used to provide the music are drums of different kinds, tambourines, bells and cymbols. The messages usually conveyed are of social issues and sex. The second type (four categories) are plays in respect of the deceased. The songs are funeral songs and songs of lamentation. Drums are the important instruments and the message conveyed is one of veneration and lamentation. The final two types are usually in worship of some deity.

Igala traditional music and dances have some distinct features. Roles for participants are well defined. Although age is not a barrier, women have different roles to play than men. In religious dances or song, men and women have separate roles and are not mixed.

TABLE 4 TYPES OF TRADITIONAL MUSIC AND DANCES

Type of Music/Dances	Function	Participants	Origin	Instruments Used
1. *Ogba*	Funeral, *Ubi*, ceremonies	Women sing; men dance	Indigenous	Drums
2. *Iyoye*	Funeral, *Ubi*, ceremonies	Women sing; men beat the drums	Indigenous	Drums,cymbals
3. *Iyogwu*	Funeral, *Ubi*, ceremonies	Women sing; men dance/ play	Indigenous	Drums

TABLE 4 TYPES OF TRADITIONAL MUSIC AND DANCES

Type of Music/Dances	Function	Participants	Origin	Instruments Used
4. *Ichabada*	Social occasions	Male and Female	*Yoruba*	Assorted drums
5. *Olele*	Social occasions	Girls only	Indigenous	Drums
6. *Agwom*	Social occasions	Women sing; men beat the drums	Indigenous	Drums
7. *Alime*	Social occasions	Male and Female	*Akpoto*	Drums
8. *Gwobe*	Social occasions	Male and Female	*Yoruba*	Drums
9. *Ibele*	Funeral	Men only	Indigenous	Drums
10. *Agale*	Funerals/ social	Men only	Indigenous	Flutes
11. *Afomi*	Funerals/ social	Only women allowed to dance	Indigenous	Drums
12. *Ogani*	Social occasions	Male	*Hausa*	Drums
13. *Igba*	Social occasions	Women sing; men dance	Indigenous	Drums
14. *Ajenuu/iye*	Religious occasions	Women only	Indigenous	Drums
15. *Idologo*	Religious occasions	Men only	Indigenous	Bells & Drums

A thorough analysis of the nature and function of Igala music and dances shows that most have to do with their social festivals. Of the fifteen different types of music and dances, only two can be directly linked to religious festivals (see Table 3). They serve the social interests of the people. People get together to interact and socialize.

Secondly, the songs and dances serve the economic interests of some people. Professional singers and dancers depend on music and dancing for their livelihood. Thirdly, some songs and dances are associated with religious rituals. People express their devotion and worship of the different deities through songs and dances. It is believed that the ancestors are made happy by the joy and happiness which typically characterizes such singing and dancing. People believe that music and dance are essential for prosperity and for receiving blessings from the ancestors.

Apart from meeting the participant's needs, music and dances give satisfaction to those who listen. That is why many donate money to singers and dancers. Politicians use singers and dancers to boost their popularity. They sing the politician's praises after he gives them money.

The Bible encourages singing and dancing in worship of God while condemning the use of music and dance for vain glory. Church planters should be open to the use of traditional music for church worship. However, experience has taught that traditional music should be introduced with biblical foundations as to its meaning, purpose, and participants.

It is also important that a study of traditional music and dance be done to determine those elements included in them by the unbelievers that must be rejected by Christians. It should not be assumed that traditional music and dance is wrong without an open-minded observation. Similarly, just because something is traditional does not make it fit for Christian worship. Each case should be examined in the light of the Scriptures with open minds and a desire for service to God.

APPLICATION: IMPLICATIONS FOR CHURCH PLANTING

As to how these leadership patterns may be adapted and applied to missionary endeavors and cross-cultural ministries the following suggestions are offered.

There is need for the church planter to be sensitive to existing leadership structures. It should be realized that even if the church succeeded in dismantling the structure on the surface, it is impossible to remove it from the cognitive domain. To this end, sensitivity towards structures will help people to adapt them and apply them in church planting and leadership development. Keeping to the existing structure helps people to relate to the customs and practices of their host. Leadership built along such structures will help the nationals to relate to each other and to accept what is presented as a non-foreign package.

It must be realized by the church planter that the dynamics of social changes affect leadership structures. While it is important that people are sensitive to existing structures and even respect such institutions, it is equally important that they are not blinded by their own theoretical biases to insist on traditional methods which are giving way to modernism. Thus, the church planter is to be sensitive enough to be open to the phenomenon of changes in the society in which the gospel is ministered. For instance, while it is true that the Igala had a centralized government system, Igala chiefs do not have much administrative and political power today with the present political set-up in Nigeria. In the same way, education and socio-economic factors have greatly influenced the descent rule. People can now set aside kinship interests and unite for material gain. Economic status is fast replacing the former royal dignity. Church planters need to see economic factors as sensitive issues rather than emphasizing the royal background of potential leaders.

There are a number of significant issues that the church planter and missions should also be sensitive to in spite of the fact that modernism has weakened tradition and the power of traditional rulers. The age factor is crucial and should be taken into consideration as people seek to train and appoint leaders. Social status on the basis of family background (royalty) and socio-economic ability are crucial to leadership selection. The church should not insist that because one has become a Christian, he should not maintain his former status. Instead, such a person should be encouraged to use his status for the good of the church. Thus, the church planter needs to recognize existing hierarchy in spite of seeming egalitarianism in modern society. Christians should not be blinded by their democratic orientation of Christian liberty and equality to undermine the impact of social distinctions. Church planters should not try to isolate the elite or royal clans from their outreach programs because they are difficult to reach or less prone to open to the gospel. The use of indigenous leadership is important. The lessons of the indirect rule of the British colonial administration should be a guide to missions, that people will in most cases feel at home with indigenous leadership instead of one imposed on them.

Chapter Six

TRADITIONALISM CONFRONTS CHRISTIANITY

THE PROBLEM OF TRADITIONALISM

Perhaps one of the problems every church planter faces is the problem of traditionalism, defined as those crucial cultural issues which Christianity confronts in any area where it is proclaimed. What are considered traditional issues in the West may not be the same in non-Western societies. For instance, in the West, church planters may have to study philosophy of religion and other philosophy-related courses in order to address Western secularism, skepticism, atheism and agnosticism, etc. These Western traditions have kept many away from the truth of the gospel.

Other Western traditions which confront Christianity are: capitalistic expansionism, which exploits the poor and needy countries of the Third World, and the manufacture and stock-piling of dangerous weapons capable of wiping out humanity from the face of the earth. Although many evangelical Christians support these Western traditions (capitalism and the arms race) as being Christian, biblical bases for supporting these traditions seems to be lacking.

Similarly, non-Western traditions which disregard the power of God for the power available through satanic means pose a threat to

Christianity. Like the Western Christian's faith in nuclear weapons for deterrence, non-Western Christians have faith in their ancestors and spirit world. Church planters should understand the problem of traditionalism faced by his receptors with the view of dealing with them biblically.

CONTEXTUAL MISSIOLOGICAL QUESTIONS

The cases given in this chapter reflect the type of traditional issues with which Western missionaries have been confronted on every field among the non-Western paganistic societies. The issues of ancestral veneration and worship, polygamy, spiritism, idolatry and traditional medicine are significant issues which the church planter must be prepared to face. Because it is impossible, I believe, to prepare answers before one goes to his field of service, it is necessary that the church planter knows the nature of traditionalism and the type of questions he will face. These general questions raise specific issues and lines of argument that are likely to be followed in an actual situation. They are:

i. Why do people go into polygamy and what needs are served? What does the Bible teach about polygamy and what sociological, psychological and moral problems are recorded in polygamous situations?
ii. How can the church help the polygamist in his Christian faith, and still not encourage his practice and life style? What is monogamy and what does the Bible say about it?
iii. How is polygamy different from multiple marriages due to constant divorce and remarriage?
iv. Who are the ancestors and how do they influence the living? What power do the ancestors have over the living Christians and what is responsible for fear and insecurity among Christians? How can the church help Christians who are afraid of the spirit world? What role should the church planter play in helping the Christians to experience the power of the Holy Spirit who is greater than all satanic spirits?
v. What is the difference between traditional medicine and Western medicine? What is the difference between

herbal medicine and processed, chemical medicine? What and who heals the sick, God or Satan? How do the church planters explain the inability of Christians to match the outworking of satanic power? How does he explain the attack of Satan on a Christian who has the Holy Spirit?

vi. What does the Bible teach about discipline, excommunication and what should the goal of the church be in administering discipline?

vii. How should the cross-cultural church planter react to the problems of traditionalism and how can he avoid seeing traditional problems through his own culture? When is the church planter wrong and when should the Bible become the final authority even when a cultural practice has to be condemned?

Problems with traditionalism will vary depending on the people involved. In the African context, however, the above questions would be helpful in understanding and dealing with the issues and problems of traditionalism.

CASE STUDY: TRADITIONALISM AMONG THE IGALA

For instance, Christian missionaries have confronted many traditional practices, *ewn ogwuchekwo,* of the Igala people and rejected them. Some of these practices are polygamy, *oya wewe,* fetishism, *ode eche,* traditional medicine, *ogwu eche,* levirate, *oya ogwu,* ancestral veneration, *abegwu kpai ubi,* drinking, *ote emo,* ceremonies involving plays and dancing, *iya ido du,* and eating the meat of animals used for sacrifice, *ela ichebo.* The missionaries taught the Igala believers to have nothing to do with these practices.

Given the Igala reliance on oral communication and history, it is impossible to document how the missionaries taught them to disregard their own cultures in order to embrace Christianity. Where evidence of such neglect and rejection of the people's culture might be found, those who control archival materials have denied the author access.

Nevertheless, evidence from personal observations and from practices arising out of what the missionaries taught abound in Igala churches today. Some of the practices forbidden by missionaries were justified. Practices that promoted immorality, idolatry and syncretism were rightly stopped. However, the missionaries went out of their way to stop other practices about which they knew very little. They forbade use of traditional medicine and traditional musical instruments. They excommunicated those found to be involved in dancing, drinking, and polygamy. Patience and systematic teaching could have probably addressed the spiritual and moral issues involved in these practices. The changes could have been volitional and from personal conviction.

Worship services had Western forms of organization and doctrines. Western music and instruments replaced the traditional ones. The Western marriage ceremony was introduced as being "civilized."

After the institutionalization of the church, some believers found that certain psychological needs were not satisfied in their newfound faith. For instance, dancing, musical instruments, and the use of traditional medicine appealed to many. With time, Christians began to go back to traditional practices when they faced life-threatening situations or significant social needs. They could not venerate their ancestors and were afraid of the spirit world. The Church began to split as the older people confronted the young people who insisted on bringing traditional musical instruments into the church.

This is the state of the Igala church today. This chapter will supply cases to reveal the nature of the present confrontation and conflict within the church. Furthermore, an analysis of these cases will show the need for the church to evaluate and expand its own theological studies. The Igala church must solve these problems by facing the challenge of traditionalism to evangelism and theology and by taking the necessary steps to address them biblically and theologically, without neglecting the Igala culture in the process.

The church planter needs to know how traditionalism has been handled in order not to underestimate its power, importance and the need for him to use the Bible and his receptor's cultures together in problem-solving strategies.

The following are cases of Igala Christians who have resorted to traditionalism. Some of these people have rejected Christianity for Islam or paganism, while others who remained have become nominal Christo-paganists, and have brought practices into the church which may be called Christian syncretism. These case studies have been arranged into four groups, each dealing with a particular traditional Igala practice. These practices are:

1) polygamy
2) ancestral veneration and worship
3) traditional medicine, and
4) pleasure-seeking issues such as drinking and dancing.

Although many cases were recorded in the research process, only a selected few will be used in this report to show the nature of the problem that is confronting Christianity among the Igala people.

POLYGAMY

Polygamy is one of the problems facing Igala Christians. Following are some of the cases recorded, showing different reasons people give for going back into polygamy. The first case shows how a Christian's desire for children could lead him into polygamy.

Case #1: **YUNUSA**

Yunusa was a pagan married to one wife before his conversion. Soon after his conversion he began to contemplate taking a second wife. He made all necessary customary arrangements for the marriage. The church was not aware of these arrangements. There was no indication that his wife was unfaithful, except that he had been under pressure from his family to take a second wife because his wife was barren.

He yielded to the pressures on him and after all the traditional marriage requirements had been met and fulfilled, Mr. Yunusa formally informed the church of his plan to take a second wife. The church's response was obviously negative. The leaders of his church tried in vain to set him straight.

When he realized that the church was not going to sanction his plan, he told the leaders that he had already made up his mind to go ahead, having concluded all necessary arrangements. The church, on hearing this, excommunicated him. Mr. Yunusa went ahead and took his second wife.

This second case has to do with a Christian whose decision to take a second wife was caused by his wife's bad conduct.

Case #2: **NOAH**

Noah became a Christian along with his wife. Both were converts from animism or paganism. But, there soon developed a serious marital problem which led Noah to decide to marry a second wife. He complained of his wife's bad conduct. The church advised him against this plan to take a second wife.

When Noah married his second wife, the church responded by excommunicating him from the fellowship. The church also advised him that in order for him to be accepted back into the fellowship, he must divorce the second wife.

This case is well over 35 years old. Mr. Noah is still under church discipline and has not been brought back into full fellowship.

These two cases show clearly how people's psycological needs drive them into polygamy. While the sexual desire of these men cannot be denied, the cases show that other needs also trigger such action. In these cases, the need for children and the alleged bad conduct of the wife were the reasons given.

The following cases definitely show the problem of polygamy prompted by sexual desire, although other reasons may have been given.

Case #3: **ANDREW**

Andrew was a Christian who had the privilege of attending a Bible school and was active in the Lord's work. He was a married man with a good family. His ministry in the church exposed him to many people and he used his position to contact those of the opposite sex. The church did not know that he was experiencing sexual temptations. When they learned, it had already degenerated into adultery.

He later took a second wife and the church followed with the excommunication order. When he realized he was excommunicated and it was unlikely that the church would rescind its order unless he divorced his second wife, he took two more wives. The church tried in vain to help him deal with his problems. Andrew is still alive and attends church services but has at least five wives.

Case #4: **JOSEPH**

Joseph was a good Christian and a dynamic preacher. He was a married man with many female children. However, in his efforts to help widows in his community, he yielded to temptation and committed adultery with a divorced Muslim woman. He later married this woman because he loved her so much and because he wanted a male child. After much futile admonition, the church excommunicated him.

Although he recognized the seriousness of his sins, Joseph refused to restore his broken fellowship. His second wife later became pregnant and bore him a male child.

Case #5: **ICHADO**

Mr. Ichado was a married man when he became a Christian. Some time after his conversion, he became ill. He consulted traditional doctors, contrary to the teachings and advice of the church. However, he was cured of the disease, said to be a poison.

After his healing, he took a second wife. When he requested baptism, the church refused on the ground of adultery, polygamy and involvement in traditional medicine. Distressed that he would not be baptized, he went into alcoholism. He remained in the church but with practically no distinction between himself and unbelievers in his life style.

ANALYSIS OF POLYGAMY CASES

These five cases have one thing in common. The first case of polygamy arose out of desire for children and the fourth case out of the desire for male children and sex. Similarly, the third and fifth cases were the result of desire for sex, while the second case arose out of the bad conduct of the wife, which the husband could not tolerate.

These Christian men have another thing in common. They knew that the church stood against their plans, but persisted to carry out their plans and desires. Even in the second case, where he informed the church, he did so only after every arrangement had been concluded.

As these men expected, the church responded in each case with an excommunication order, following admonition to stop their plans or put away such second wives. It should be realized that these men claim to be Christians and were in some ways active in their respective churches before their decision to take additional wives. The decision of the church to excommunicate them was based on the church's doctrine of monogamy, and not necessarily based on actual individual cases.

However, these cases have shown that Christians go into polygamy as a result of some perceived needs and pressures from their families to meet certain expectations. They also show that life-threatening situations were not causes of polygamous marriages in these cases. Perhaps it would be better if the whole issue of traditional marriage and polygamy be addressed in the doctrine of the church so that the Igala Christians might see the Biblical and theological implications of this practice. Such teaching through dialogue and intense study may result in a sound doctrine based on the Scriptures and the Igala practice.

ANCESTORS: VENERATION, RITUALS AND WORSHIP

Perhaps the most serious obstacle that is keeping Igalas from embracing Christianity is the fear that their ancestors will be neglected or disregarded. Christians who are faced with life-threatening issues turn often to ancestor veneration. There are at least five important benefits the Igala derive from their ancestors:

1) Peace — the security of not being disturbed by the spirits of the dead
2) Prosperity — Protection from bad omens
3) Longevity of life — The prevention of diseases
4) Protection — The revelation of secret harmful plans against someone
5) Social acceptance — The restoration of credibility

These are perceived needs which the Igala believe the ancestors provide. In order for one to be assured of these benefits or blessings, the one interested must perform *Ibegwu* ritual and *Ubi* festival. These are the two main ceremonies in which the ancestors are addressed or propitiated.

Ancestral veneration is so important and crucial to the Igala that even Christians will either renounce their faith in favor of it or become involved in Christian syncretism — practicing ancestral veneration while at the same time remaining a Christian. The Igala church generally will not accommodate such syncretistic practices and those found involving themselves in ancestral veneration and ritual are often excommunicated. In spite of the reaction of the church to this practice, some Christians whose needs are being met in this practice prefer the discipline of the church to that of the ancestors, and so remain in syncretism.

In addition to the above benefits, it has been said that when fertility rituals are performed to them, the ancestors can intercede for the concerned parties. Social acceptance is another reason why some Christians get involved. This is especially true of the *Ubi* festival. The prestige or status of older Christian women is determined by the *Ubi* festival.

The following cases show the extent of this problem among the Igala Christians. These cases also show the need for the church to address this issue for the benefit of the those who might be tempted to practice these rituals as well as those who have already become involved.

Case #6: **AKOWE**

Akowe was the firstborn of his parents. Being the firstborn, he was expected to be the head of the family at the death of his father. As head of the family, it was his responsibility to organize and discharge all religious, social and family rituals in accordance with tradition.

However, Mr. Akowe became a Christian and as such was expected to do away with his paganistic and traditional rituals. He stopped performing the rituals and sacrifices to the ancestors. This negligence led his family members to prevail on him to denounce Christianity or at least remain faithful to the spirit of the ancestors.

He yielded to the pressures put on him by resorting to practice of ancestral veneration and associated rituals. The church, on hearing this, advised him to distance himself from traditionalism — to no avail. Mr. Akowe, while remaining in the church, refused to take a firm stand for Christ. Instead he prefers to be called a

Christian and at the same time be involved in ancestral veneration.

Case #7: **IDAKWO**

Idakwo was a pagan before his conversion to Christ. He was also a polygamist and a drunkard. When he became a Christian, the church admonished him about his drinking habit, but he would not give it up.

There came a time when he fell sick and was close to death. His relatives told him that the cause of his sickness was his neglect of the ancestors since he had become a Christian. When he heard this, he made up his mind to renounce Christianity. When the church learned of it, efforts were made to make him realize that dead ancestors had no power to cause him harm. But, he left the church and has never returned. He was afraid that the ancestors would kill him if he remained in the church.

Case #8: **DANIEL**

When Daniel became a Christian, he looked promising. He became involved in a number of church activities. However, not long after his conversion, he started to fornicate, drink and participate in the ancestor's rituals.

Because of his involvement in fornication and drinking, he became afraid of being killed by poison. This fear led him to embrace fetishism and ancestral rituals. His belief was that the ancestors will offer him protection. In all these he remained in the church, unconcerned and unrepentant. He does not see why ancestral rituals should affect his relationship to Christ.

This sixth case has to do with the need for one to be faithful to his ancestors. It illustrates how Christians are put under pressure to do what is important and crucial to their families. People get into ancestral practices because of fear and the need for protection from sickness. The ancestors are believed to be very powerful and protective. The fear of being poisoned is another factor which often takes people into ancestral veneration. This need for protection from evil spirits led Daniel into the ancestral rituals. For Ahiaba and his wife, their need for children was great. They were told that the ancestors could help them.

Case #9: **AHIABA**

Ahiaba and his wife were Christians. Their children all died in infancy, however, and they were very much concerned about it. Their families advised them to offer some sacrifices to the ancestors in order to have their blessing. They were also to go to the native doctor for native medication. They wrestled with these for sometime. It was a difficult time in their lives, as these practices were not sanctioned by their church.

On the one hand, the pressure to have children was on them. The church advised them to keep trusting the Lord for the blessing of children. Disturbed by the fact that without children, he would have no representative in his paternal lineage, Ahiaba decided to perform the rituals prescribed and to visit native doctors for medication.

After a short while, his wife became pregnant and bore a child which lived. From this point on, all their children lived. Even though the church put them out of fellowship, the leaders could not say much since native medication had helped the couple.

Ancestral veneration is believed to be a way to appease them. Some people venerate the ancestors because they want to go to the ancestor's feet at death. The following case illustrates this.

Case #10: **EJIMA**

It was the desire of Ejima, on becoming a Christian, to remain in a few traditional festivals. He wanted to keep the Ibegwu festival in which the ancestors are remembered and venerated. Secondly, he wanted his family members to perform his death ritual, *Ubi* festival. The church told him not to fear the ancestors but he would not listen.

He specifically requested that his family members perform the *Ubi* festival to enable him to go safely to the feet of his ancestors. A few months later he died and his family performed the ritual he had so longed for. This incidence disturbed the church greatly. The church felt that his conversion experience was probably not a genuine one.

The need for protection and social acceptance drives others to ancestral veneration and rituals.

Case #11: **OMEHI**

Omehi was saved while attending a mission hospital. She was moved to accept Christ because of the loving care of the missionaries working at the medical center where she spent a number of years suffering from leprosy.

When she was cured of her leprosy, she returned home to be with her people. Her relatives were surprised that she had become a Christian. They were concerned that she would no longer be involved in traditional practices. They were even more concerned that the *Ubi* festival would not be allowed at her funeral.

Omehi listened to the complaints of her people. She was particularly concerned that she would not see her fathers (ancestors) if the *Ubi* festival was not performed. To convince her family members of her decision to get back into these rituals, she left the church. (She knew the church would not accommodate these ideas.) When she died, she was buried according to the traditional rites.

In review, the need for children is crucial among the Igala Christians. Many Christians who cannot have children either resort to polygamy (case #1) or ancestral ritual (case #9). In some cases Christians are under pressure from their family members to consult their ancestors and use traditional medicines in order to get their wishes. That is what happened to Ahiaba and his wife (case #9).

Ejima (case #10) needed security and assurance which can be found only in Christ. Instead, he believed that such security could be secured from ancestors. He did not want to rely completely on Christ. In the case of Omehi (case #11), she wanted to be socially accepted by her people and she thought that she needed the ancestors badly. It seems that she failed to understand her privileges and completeness in Christ.

The need for protection from evil spirits is also a crucial one. Not only do people seek protection for themselves, they are expected to protect their family members as well. This case shows that problem.

Case #12: **BABA**

Baba, a young Christian man, was the father of four daughters.

He and his wife were looking for a son badly and God provided a son. However, this infant had curly hair. In Igala society when a child is born with curly hair, it is believed that the child is *Ichekpa*. This means that the Ichekpa spirit must be consulted and sacrificed to from time to time. It is also believed that the hair must not be shaved without the consent of the child and that if a haircut is given without the child's consent, he will die.

This belief is not held by the church. The church leaders instructed Baba to shave his son. Baba held that his child would die and he did not want to kill him. The church refused to see things from Baba's perspective, and since Baba refused to do what he was told, he was excommunicated. The church held that the boy's hair is a symbol of shame and disgrace. Furthermore, it shows that the Ichekpa spirit can indwell a Christian, which the church denies. The church also held that Baba's deliberate refusal to give his child a haircut shows that he was afraid of the spirit and was not grateful for God's gift of a child.

On the other hand, Baba maintained that he would be guilty of killing his son if he went ahead and gave him a haircut.

In the end, however, this child grew up and demanded to have a haircut. It was done and he is still alive. Baba is still under discipline, about fifteen years after this incident. He maintained that his excommunication was unjustified. The church also maintains that he will not be restored into fellowship without repentance. He is farther from the faith than he was when the church excommunicated him. And the church has not made any attempt to bring him back into full fellowship.

ANALYSIS OF CASES OF ANCESTRAL RITUALS

These seven cases involve the veneration of the ancestors and participation in their rituals. Each case represents a perceived need for which Igala Christians turned to the ancestors. Because these needs are very crucial to Igala people, when the church fails to supply adequate answers, people turn to traditional means.

The church reacted by confronting, persuading and finally excommunicating the people involved. The church did not offer any viable alternatives and thus failed to impact these people. Their needs were not addressed by the church and further, the church leaders reprimanded them for their practices. These people have been in the church and probably know the consequences of their actions. But what they need is not someone to remind them of how wrong they were. They need to be shown an alternative Christian method of meeting their need of security, good health and protection from the evil spirits. This the church failed to offer.

To these people, something which was obviously lacking in the church was available to them elsewhere. They had the assurance of the ancestors and they accept and believe what they have been taught and what they have experienced.

Christians, it seems, have become indifferent to the realities of the ancestral world. They have been taught by their leaders to disregard the spirit world. This is evidenced in the lack of teaching on this subject in theological studies. These cases should convince the church of the importance of the ancestral world so that the subject should be addressed in theological studies. Understanding gained from systematic studies will help the church in evangelizing those still under allegiance to the ancestors and as well as those weak Christians who still venerate the ancestors out of fear, intimidation and lack of understanding of their own resources in Christ.

TRADITIONAL MEDICINE AND DOCTORS

The need for good health and security is a serious and crucial one for all people. This need cuts across sex and age barriers. The Igala people have a strong belief in herbal medicine. Before the coming of Christianity, traditional medicine (a combination of herbs and other ingredients) were used as a prevention and cure. This was often done by traditional doctors, sorcerers or diviners. In many instances, traditional medicine was associated with sorcery and religious rituals. Whatever form it took, one thing was clear. People were getting healed and protection from the attacks of medicine men was guaranteed.

When the missionaries came to introduce Christianity to the Igala and the church was established, the believers were taught that traditional medicine was evil, and Western medicine was introduced. It must be conceded that medical missions helped the Igala people immensely, as God used these missionaries who had little medical training to bring healing to many people. Furthermore, most of the Igala people who accepted Christianity did so because of the exposure to the gospel through the medical work.

Despite these successes, Western medicine could not cure all the diseases of the people. Diseases are believed to have spiritual origin and no medication could solve such spiritual problems. The Igala people believe that spiritual issues in sickness should be addressed spiritually. Western medication does not have the power to deal with such cases.

In several cases, people were brought to the orthodox doctors, but they could not see any physical problem, though the patient was obviously in pain. Such cases take spiritual medication for healing. Since these cases cannot be understood by Western missionaries and medicine, they are frowned upon.

The Igala Christians are faced with this serious dilema of whether to disregard traditional medicine in favor of Western medicine. On the other hand, they have seen the weakness of Western medicine in cases where their traditional medicine could have brought healing. Because of the fear of being excommunicated, these Christians secretly resort to traditional practices when faced with sickness.

The following cases (#13 and 14) will show how two Christians received healing from traditional doctors and subsequently renounced their faith. Other cases (#15, 16, 17) concern the Christians' quest for some protection through the use of fetishes and charms instead of putting their trust in Christ. This concern is borne out by the proverb which says, "One does not open his door for God to shut or close." In other words, man must seek to protect himself. God may be too busy to get involved in such petty details. These cases reveal that desire in people to help themselves.

Case #13: MOSES

Moses was a Christian and in fellowship (communicant). When he became ill, the church went to pray for him. The sickness would not go away. He was receiving treatment at a local hospital and there was nothing else the church could do.

When his condition deteriorated, he went to seek the help of native doctors. The native doctors used herbs, charms and other ingredients in treating Moses. After a short period with the native doctor, he was cured and became well again. However, he became a Muslim following his discharge because he knew he had violated the church law which prevents Christians from receiving native medicine and doctors.

Case #14: **ADIJA**

Adija was a devout Christian but her husband was not. She became ill and, after all the church prayers had failed to produce healing, she was taken to a native doctor by her unbelieving husband. She was there for a long time and was finally healed. On returning home, she renounced her faith and became a pagan. Her reason was that Christianity was not able to heal her. She thought it would be reasonable to worship the gods that gave her healing.

On the other hand, Adija's unbelieving husband became a Christian. His own reason for becoming a Christian was because of the miraculous healing of his wife. And although he tried to win his wife back to the faith, she refused to return to Christ.

ANALYSIS OF CASES OF TRADITIONAL MEDICINE

These two people who claimed to be Christians, when faced with death or life-threatening situations, decided to seek out traditional sources of help in order to survive.

The church, confronted with these situations, prayed, but, these people were not healed. Because the church believed in Western medicine, they will not allow these patients to seek the help of traditional doctors.

When they realized that the church could offer no hope or help, the people involved decided to consult traditional doctors, who were able to help them. After their healing, they left the church because they realized that the church would respond by excommunicating them and also that the church did not have power to protect them.

These cases discredited the church in that the traditional doctors were seen to have more power than the Christian God. They also reveal the necessity for the Igala Christians to know the distinction between traditional medicine using spiritual means, and the use of traditional medicine using herbal means. It is important that a thorough study of ethnomedicine be undertaken, with the aim of making this distinction possible. Such studies could be a subject which theological education could effectively address.

SECURITY AND POWER

Cases #15, 16, and 17 show the Igala people's need for security. The cases reveal how far Christians can go to seek for protection, security and power, due to their fear and lack of faith in God.

Case #15: ANAJA

Anaja was a young Christian who demonstrated some signs of spiritual growth immediately following his conversion. He was a driver and had seen automobile accidents resulting in death. He was advised by his friends to get some fetishes which would enable him to disappear or get out of a vehicle in times of accident. This fetish is believed by most unbelieving drivers to be efficacious. Fear for his life and need for security drove Anaja into idolatry. In spite of the admonition of the church, Anaja renounced Christianity. He realized that his new practices were incompatible with Christianity and so decided to go into Islam.

Case #16 SIMON

Simon was a good Christian who was in the pastorate for some years. However, he fell into sexual sin and was excommunicated. Because of the nature of his sin, flirting and having relations with other men's wives, he decided to seek medicine and fetishes with which to protect himself from the attacks of his rivals and enemies.

Although Simon is still in the church, he has his hands in polygamy, witchcraft and native medicine. He could not trust and believe God to help him get over his problems and security needs.

Case #17: ALI

Ali was a good Christian until he became involved in several land disputes. In Igala culture, land is very important and when one is involved in a land dispute, he is said to be sticking his head out.

Having realized that he had made enemies in most of his land cases, he sought traditional medicine and fetishes with which to protect himself. In addition to self-defense, he became involved in charming people with the intent to do harm to them.

When it became known that he was involved in spiritism, he left the church. The church's effort to reason with him fell on deaf ears.

ANALYSIS OF SECURITY AND POWER CASES

The basic problem in these three cases is that of security. The man in case #15 wanted power to overcome spirits that cause accidents on the highway. In case #16, the man was in need of the power to protect his life from the attacks of his enemies (those with whose wives he was having sexual relations). Similarly the man in case #17, who was involved in several land cases or disputes, wanted power to win his court cases and provide security from the attacks of his enemies.

These men knew very well that the church would not permit this practice and so decided to leave the church. These cases show that these believers did not know of the power of Christ and so opted for what evil spirits could offer them. If they had seen the dynamism of the church, especially in responding to spiritual attacks on Christians, perhaps they would have been more inclined to think through their actions.

It is important to stress that while these men knew the power of traditional medicine (fetishes) because they were saved out of animism, there is a need for the church to teach them from the scriptural standpoint. To deny their existence, as has been the case, will not solve this problem.

DRINKING AND TRADITIONAL MUSIC

Cases #18, 19, and 20 deal with three different issues that Igala Christians constantly face, the problem of drinking, traditional dancing and singing, and of taking a fellow Christian to court.

Case #18: **Ebilayi**

This case involves a Christian man called Ebilayi. His main problem was the drinking of alcohol. This habit degenerated into drunkeness. Mr Ebilayi's church was against this habit and decided to preach against it. In their messages, drunkeness was condemned. The church would not compromise on this issue and systematic Bible teaching was presented on this subject. When Mr. Ebilayi was tired of listening to condemnatory messages castigating his habit of drinking, he left the church. He was not prepared to stop drinking.

Case #19: **MARY**

Mary was a Christian lady who was very interested in singing and dancing. When this was introduced in the church, she became very active and was fully involved in the church choir. However, the missionaries later decided that it was wrong to allow drumming and dancing in the church since it was practiced by the pagans. When Mary discovered that the church could no longer accept dancing and the use of traditional musical instruments, she left the church and became a pagan. She renounced her faith on the grounds that traditional music and dance were not allowed in worship.

ANALYSIS OF CASES OF DRINKING AND TRADITIONAL MUSIC

These problems are common, but are smaller issues than earlier cases. However, they reveal personal crises in Christian lives, and how the church has closed itself to issues of importance.

In case #18, Mr Ebilayi knew well the church's stand against drunkenness. However, the church's constant condemnation and preaching against this practice from the pulpit angered him. He left the church as a result.

Case #19 involves forbidding the use of traditional musical instruments and dances in worship. When Mary realized that the church would not open to the traditional music, she left the church. The church's action to stop the use of traditional musical instruments has not been rescinded.

These cases show the failure of the church to understand the serious nature of the problems involved. Perhaps these problems could have been solved if the church had been open to discussion and treated each case meritoriously.

Contemporary church planter has a responsibility to study and understand how christianity impacts traditionalism. To deny the nature of traditionalism and how it is confronting biblical christianity is a mere cop out. The threat which syncretism and idolatory pose to the expansion of biblical christianity is devastating. Understanding its impacts and consequences to the church planting process is crucial. The church planter is called to recognizc thc impacts and implications to his ministry and receptors. He also is called to stick to the Bible and the realities of context factor.

Chapter Seven

CONTEMPORARY SOCIETY AND CULTURAL CHANGE

Great changes are occurring in the twentieth century. These changes affect everyone in every culture, regardless of whether or not they are noticed. However, where changes are noticed, people tend to chase shadows or blame others for them. In many developing countries, where Christian missionaries from the West have worked alongside colonial governments, missionaries have been accused of changing the people's cultures. While European and Christian missionaries can be held responsible for some changes that occurred in some non-Western cultures, they cannot be held exclusively responsible for all changes.

Cultural change is inevitable. Changes can be attributed to the worldwide penetration of Western culture and Western education, migration, the coming of missionaries, nationalism and other accompanying factors such as urbanization, industrialization and diversification of economic activities in many societies. Therefore, it should be realized that no one can stop the phenomenon of social change, and one person should not be held responsible for such social changes.

Those involved in church planting should not assume that cross-cultural training would help them to maintain traditional society and thus be free from accusations of changing the people's culture. It is impossible for church planters, as agents of change, not to have influence on the receptor's culture. A role of the church planter is to help people adjust to changes. Church planters can also use in their outreach the positive elements brought about by changes instead of feeling guilty for being part of the changes in the receptor's society.

CONTEXTUAL MISSIOLOGICAL QUESTIONS

The theory of social change has become an acceptable one in the social sciences. Even structural-functionalists who traditionally denied the possibility of cultural change are no longer able to present any convincing and acceptable argument against the theory of social change.

Structural-functionalists have for so many years singled out missionaries, accused them and held them in contempt for changing the cultures of people among whom they work. These accusations no longer carry any weight as other factors can equally be said to have contributed to social changes in most contemporary societies.

Today's church planter who has had the opportunity of receiving prefield cross-cultural training often goes to the field with the notion that he is a catalyst who has nothing to do with his receptor's culture. Accepting the accusations against the pioneer missionaries by some anthropologists, contemporary missionaries think that it is possible for them to go into a culture and remain neutral. Some even try to take their receptors back into their traditional practices as if they can right the wrong done by the Westernization of the people at the expense of their own traditions.

Contemporary missionaries and church planters need to realize that they are agents of change. They will definitely influence some changes in the receptors' culture knowingly or unknowingly. Furthermore, the issue of social change is one that no one has control over as changes are inevitable. It will be a waste of effort to try to remain neutral. Rather, cross-cultural church planters should understand the nature of the theory of social change, and identify the types of changes, causes and how people react to them within the socio-cultural setting of their ministry. There is no need for anyone to feel guilty for changes taking place in traditional societies. A thorough understanding of what elements or factors are responsible for such changes would help the church planter invaluably in his ministry with his receptors.

The church planter needs to ask some questions in regard to the changes evidenced in the cultures of his receptors. Such questions may help him better analyze the problems, issues and advantages of contemporary social changes and their consequential effects on church planting. There is need to ask:

1. What areas or spheres of people's culture are vulnerable to changes? How do people react to changes? What are the causes of changes and who are held responsible by those experiencing them?
2. Who are those who favor or are against social changes? What effect has economics on social changes? Has the coming of Christianity anything to do with changes? How is Christianity perceived among the receptors in relation to changes?
3. What is the effect of social changes on religion? How does the church benefit from social changes? In what ways can the church help or discourage certain social changes?
4. The church planter needs to look at his own culture and study how social changes take place, if any. He also needs to realize that his own culture and types of changes may be different from those of his receptors.

CASE STUDY: CULTURAL CHANGE AMONG THE IGALA

In fact, among the Igala people the contemporary society has undergone many changes. It is not difficult to find how far these changes have affected the foundation of the structure of the society. The changes taking place are mainly in the family, social, and political structures. It should be realized that the changes are caused by education, urbanization, industrialization and by Christian factors. Although the main compulsive factor is economic, Christianity paved the way for these factors.

A thorough analysis of contemporary changes reveals that people are more than willing to accept changes as long as their economic interests are served. They also accept changes because their economic resources are producing an incredible amount of power with which to control people. These changes affect the traditional beliefs and practices of the Igala people.

TYPES OF CHANGES IN FAMILY STRUCTURE

Structural changes are taking place in Igala society today. These changes in the Igala family structure has been caused by economic problems and interests. In order to support the view that structural changes are taking place, it is necessary to study cases of such events. The following are areas where such changes have occurred in the family structure. The cases illustrate the particular changes taking place.

Case #1: AUTHORITY AND CONFLICT IN FATHER-SON RELATIONS

Sule left his village in search of a factory job in a city after finishing his primary education. In the city, he lived with his parallel cousin Ida. Ida has a family of four and was not making enough money. When Sule came, his problem increased as he would be responsible for his food, board and helping him get a job.

Ida succeeded in getting a factory job for Sule and Sule rented an apartment for himself. Having become independent and with a job, he began to support his poor parents in the village monthly. He also was financing the education of his younger brothers. His parents were proud of him because of the manner in which he was helping the family.

However, not long after that, Sule fell in love with a girl he met in the city who was from a different tribe. Without consulting his own parents or the girl's, he married her and they lived together as husband and wife.

Soon after their marriage, his relationship to his family began to change. He could not send money home regularly and was not able to provide for his brothers' education. When the parents demanded to know what was wrong, Sule explained that he had a wife and a small baby to take care of. His parents were very upset about this development. They were surprised and unhappy that Sule would marry a girl from an entirely different tribe.

Sule's wife works too and this affected her relationship with her own family. Because of the nature of her job, Sule helps to look after the baby when he is off duty. In addition, he cooks whenever she is away at work. These practices were perfectly acceptable to both of them since they are looking for the best for their own family.

One day, Sule's father decided to visit his son to see things for himself. On arrival, he met Sule's wife and having introduced himself, he was asked to sit down and feel at home. But Sule's father could not speak English and so was unable to communicate with his daughter-in-law without a translator. As Sule and his father sat to discuss family matters, Sule discovered that his family was upset and not supportive of his marriage. He too was unhappy that his family would not sympathize with him.

During this visit, Sule's father took note of a number of issues. Apart from the main issue of a non-Igala wife, Sule would call his wife "dear" and would seek his wife's opinion on most issues. To complicate the matter, Sule was seen caring for the baby and cooking the food whenever she went away to work. When she was home, all the family members, including the wife and Sule's father would eat at the same table. These changes were too much for the old man to stomach.

Before leaving for the village, he explained to Sule that he was not considered to be their son anymore because of the betrayal of his family. Sule's father explained further that his act had brought shame on his own family. Sule was devastated by these statements, but he could not make any response. His father left with sadness and disappointment.

This case shows the nature of conflict existing between parents and their children. Sule should have been under the control of his father. He should not have married without his father's consent. Neither should he have dreamed of marrying someone from another tribe entirely. The same thing applied to Sule's wife. She went the way of modernity. Sule's father observed a number of dynamics. First of all, he saw the change in his authority and the role of his child.

In the past, Igala culture defined children as properties of the father. Children were therefore provided for and used on the farm by their parents. In old age, they provide security for their parents. Children were expected to live with their aging parents or at least take them to live with themselves. Aging parents were not to live by themselves. This is changing rapidly. Parents still expect their children to provide for them. But, because of education, children no longer work on the farm. They are not expected to live with their parents because of their desire to raise a separate family, to live in the cities, and to provide money instead of personal labor. Children no longer want to be told what to do but want to run their own lives. This development has not only affected the parent-child relationship but also the morality of children. Brown (1983) shows sexual promiscuity in children and the existence of single women with illegitimate children. Parents no longer have direct control over their children due to urbanization and industrialization (Uzoka 1980). Children also make decisions as to when to marry, who to marry and how to marry (Culinovic 1983), (Ngwisha 1978) and dictate the type of parent-children relationship (Flanagàn 1977), (Vellenga 1975) they will have.

It can be seen, therefore, that the changing role of children in Igala family structure over time has been caused by urbanization, education, influence of Western culture, migration and quest for egalitarianism. These causes have been triggered by economic interests.

Secondly, he observed the role of his daughter-in-law in relation to domestic activities. He discovered that Sule was sharing her domestic work, a reversal of the traditionally valued sex role.

In a traditional Igala family structure, women were to be seen and not heard. Women's roles were limited to child bearing and rearing and domestic responsibilities like cooking, washing and working on the farm. In most cases they were regarded as the husband's personal property. As long as she was alive she belonged to her husband and, at the death of the husband, to the husband's family. It was the responsibility of the husband to provide everything the wife needed in return.

However, this arrangement does not seem to hold any more due to economic changes. The husband with his many wives and children and extended family members and their responsibilities is beginning to face the challenges of modernity and can no longer provide the former traditional security for the woman. The inability of the man to provide for the family sufficiently has led many women to find alternative ways to fend for themselves and their children.

The influence of Western culture and education has contributed immensely to the changing role of women in Igala society. Today, women are seen, are heard, and are providing for their families. This is common in modern societies. It cannot be denied that economic implications convinced Igala men that women have more to offer than child bearing, rearing and cooking. Callaway (1984) shows the traditional role of women in Islamic societies is in no way representative of the dynamic changes occurring in most Nigerian cultures today. For instance, Okonjo (1976) shows in his study of Igbo women in Nigeria that migration, education and religion have affected family life through changes in the roles of women and that changes will be accepted if they are economically and socially rewarding. Bellenga (1975) shows the changing sex roles in Ghana and how women are becoming more independent with their children because they (women) are able to provide the economic power. Similarly, Amobi (1980) observes that the education of the wife has a negative effect on her fertility as she begins to work and contribute to the family income, her primary traditional role of child bearing changes and her husband has to look at her differently. Sacks (1971) found that women's participation in collective social labor is the economic base for an adult social status for women (that is their ability to engage in egalitarian relations with other adults in the society). She also observes that in Ghana, a class society where women are domestic producers only, they lack rights which women at Mbuti, Louedu, and Pondo had because they engage in collective social production.

Women's new roles include the right to determine the family size (Benoit, Levi and Vimard 1986), the right to be involved in economic activities (Davis 1983), (Sudarkasa 1982), (Due and Summary 1982) and the right to be themselves and act independently. Many other studies have shown that changes may be slow (Mikell 1984), (Rizika; Sleady; Chiepe; Rogombe 1985), that sexism still pervades (Ferrier 1983), (McCrea 1983), (Due 1982) but will definitely argue for dynamic changes over time (Oke 1986).

In Igala culture, gender and age play major roles and are factors guiding social behavior, interactions and activities. Men and women have specific roles and responsibilities. Children and adults have their own roles and responsibilities. These distinctions are giving way to changing roles for women and children in many African societies as shown in studies done by Rizika (1985), Sleady (1985), Rogombe (1985), Chiepe (1985), Amobi (1980), Benoit, Levi and Vimard (1986), and Okonjo (1976), Vellenga (1975).

In Igala society, children and women are becoming very powerful and important because of their economic power and support for the family. Education has provided women and young men opportunities to do what was traditionally the exclusive responsibility of males and adults. Since such assumption of responsibilities means economic relief for the males and adults, it is acceptable — and thus removes the age-long gender and age distinction traditions.

Other aspects of change in family structure are the issues of early marriages, polygamy and family planning. The case below illustrates the problems that people are facing in today's society in relation to the issues involved.

Case #2: **MONOGAMY AND FAMILY PLANNING**

Mudi was a well educated man and was thought to be very intelligent and responsible. He also had a good job. When he decided to marry his family was so happy. With his family's backing and support, he married a young educated lady from his tribe. This also pleased his parents.

However, soon after their marriage, she went back to her former job in a town which was about two hundred miles away. This was a temporary arrangement until she was able to get a local job near Mudi. The parents of Mudi were not happy with this arrangement. In the end, the two got together and lived together, to the relief of Mudi's parents.

About six months after their wedding, Mudi's wife was not pregnant. His family was concerned. They asked their son what was happening. To their astonishment, they were told that Mudi

> and his wife were practicing family planning. This means that they would have children when they were able to raise them well and that they planned to have only three children. These facts did not go well with the parents of either the bride or the groom.
>
> Mudi's parents thought that Mudi could afford a second wife and so were going to talk him into it, but could not when they were told of their son's plan to have only one wife and three children. In spite of the pressures from his peers, family members and parents-in-law, Mudi and his wife refused to oblige.

Mudi's decision not to marry earlier was his desire for economic security. After acquiring his education, with his family's support, he married a young educated girl. However, they had to make decisions which were economic in nature. The wife must return to work; there was a plan to have only three children and a firm commitment to monogamy. In spite of the pressures from many quarters, Mudi and his wife refused to change their decisions.

In 1983, there was a severe drought for a year in Northern Nigeria, and it was reported that many polygamists got divorced because they could no longer provide food for every member of the family. Studies have also shown that Western education has influenced people to set some new and different value standards. With these set of new value standards, including the education of children to the highest possible level, people are beginning to question the economic possibilities of polygamy. It can be seen that the deciding factor is economic. According to Ugwuegbu, Western educated Nigerian men and women tend to develop close-mindedness to polygamy (Ugwuegbu 1982:151). Researchers have also shown the impact of the transformation of family structure over time (Demos 1970) and the serious effects of urbanization and industrialization on family functions (Uzoka 1980). Laslett and Wall (1972) have also noticed transformation in family structure.

For the average Igala man, his appetite for many children, for sex, and male children are being curbed. The oil revenue from which everyone amasses wealth is dwindling (Barbar 1982) and polygamy can only thrive on a sound economic base (Amobi 1980). Brown's studies of Botswana (1983) reveals that economic problems which led people to migrate have discouraged polygamy and encouraged spacing children.

It has been the practice of the Igala people to marry early in life. While marriageable ages are not fixed, it is observed that female children are given in marriage at puberty and male children expected to marry when they become sexually productive. The only exception has been the quest of Western education which is delaying many early marriages.

However, it has been observed that early marriages among the Igala people are no longer ideal. This is because of the financial obligations involved. Young people are craving for education which will enhance their economic status. This development, coupled with the new value systems, have led many young people to put off early marriages. The postponement has introduced problems such as premarital sexual relations, migration, abortion and sometimes the birth of illegitimate children. Brown (1983) observes in her research in Botswana, South Africa, that evidence shows that high male out-migration has led to a modification in the structure of family life and has transformed women's social and economic positions to their detriment (Brown 1983:367). Studies show that economic problems led to migration and thereby cause significant changes such as: delayed marriage until a later age — about 30 or over.

Early marriage is no longer possible, and courting relations and love affairs now flourish. Men marry at 30 and above instead of at 20. Sexual promiscuity and children out of the bond of marriage are common. This study by Barbara Brown of the people of Botswana reveals the very problem of Igala people today. Changes in household structure have occurred as a result of new patterns of marriage. A significant number of women never marry. In addition, the existence of households headed by single women represents a major change in the social and economic structure of rural Botswana (Brown 1983:375).

The Igala family structure is fast changing because of the absence of early marriages which have triggered a number of other economic and social maladies. Uzoka shows that it leads to lack of control over children (Uzoka 1980) and changes in family structure in relation to relationships, wedding customs and social customs

(Culinovic 1983). In his research in Zambia, Ngwisha observes, too, that economic problems resulting in urbanization have created a tendency towards permissiveness in the parent-child relationship (Ngwisha 1978), and this permissiveness goes even to the issue of early marriages (Vellenga 1975).

The concept of birth control and family size is unfamiliar in Igala culture. To the Igala, the primary purpose of marriage is procreation. No limit should be set by way of family planning. It implies, then, that wives are to bear or produce as many children as they are given by God, and when the number given by God is not satisfactory, the man may go into polygamous marriages to increase the family size. Over the years, economic problems have been altering this world view. Food shortages as a result of prolonged drought, the demand for Western education for children, and the demand for material things for family members have adversely affected the Igala traditional belief in a large family.

These economic factors led the government to issue a strong appeal to the Igala people to control their family size. The people have also seen their economic inadequacies, the changing roles of women and children, and the ecological factors that have changed their occupational activities and production of food. The Igala is forced by his dilemmas to look at the economics of child bearing. This is true of many other third world nations. Tuladhar (1981) observes in studies from Nepal that economic problems pushed the government to introduce family planning. This government program was observed to be effective, though urban women who are educated and are working tend to have been more open to it. This is supported by Brown (1983) whose studies of rural Bostwana people have shown that economic problems resulting into out migration has led to spacing of children among the Tswana tribe.

Economic problems not only dictate family size (Liker and Elder 1983) they also determine the quality of food consumed by families (Morgan, Johnson and Burt 1983).

While in India, some people are still opposed to family planning (Verna 1984), it cannot be denied that economic problems are the primary concern of proponents of family planning. According to Fosu (1986), family planning as a challenge to economic problems is well received and in practice in Accra, Ghana. Studies of the developing economies of Kenya and Nigeria (Amobi 1980) reveal that family income influences family size. This study was supported by Dmereuwaonu (1977) who shows that family planning can limit the size of the family because of economic crises.

The concept of extended family relationship is fast changing. In the case below, Musa who resides in an urban setting decided, when he was getting married, not to allow any of his family and extended family members to live with him.

Case #3: **NUCLEAR FAMILY CONCEPT**

Musa was a soldier who was stationed about five hundred kilometers away from home. Musa came home twice, when he was about to prepare for the appointment of a go-between and during the engagement.

Then, after all arrangements for his wedding were completed, he came home to take his wife away to live. Nobody quarreled with him about patrilocal residence since he was a member of the working class and did not live at home (his village). However, two things happened. First, his mother-in-law told him to take one of the bride's sisters along to raise, as was the Igala practice. Musa said that he would not be able to raise anybody else. This provoked his in-laws and the matter was reported to the go-between. Secondly, after settling with his wife, his own father came with Musa's younger brother and told him that, being the first born, he must look after the younger children. Musa was also reminded of the fact that they (the parents) were getting old and would soon become inactive.

Having listened to his father, he responded gently that he realized that it was his responsibility to take care of the family members, but he could not offer to help his brother now because he was facing serious economic problems and the boy might not get along with his wife. In the end his father returned to the village with his son.

Musa's economic problems and his interest in his wife led him to decide not to open his house to his extended family members.

As strong and as important as the Igala extended family structure was, changes have taken place. These changes have given different definitions to the concept of extended family.

The extended family relationship has been narrowed so that very close kinsmen are recognized. In addition while relationship is maintained, economic help is no longer required, but desired. Another change is in its relationship to urbanization. It has been widely believed that urbanization has been detrimental to extended family structure. However, studies have shown the contrary. Ngwisha (1978) has shown that urbanization has not destroyed extended family structure. In fact, Flanagan (1977) observes that the extended family unit promotes urbanization. Urbanization itself changes the formal or traditional family structure in that family members are no longer together but scattered. It is important to point out here that the changes initiated as a result of urbanization have given new definition to the extended family unity. It is this belief that prompts Ngwisha (1978) to conclude that urbanization has not destroyed extended family structure.

To be more precise, it is essential to say that while the extended family has been scattered due to urbanization (Flanagan 1977), new relationships have been developed. Relatives living in urban areas are still responsible to provide economic help in the form of monthly living allowances and sponsorship of relatives at schools in the rural areas. This keeps the relationship intact and on-going. In addition, it can be seen that young high school graduates go to cities to live with extended family members in search of factory or industry jobs (Ngwisha 1978).

Thus, it can be said that economic changes have greatly influenced the Igala extended family structure. It has given it new scope, definition, purpose, and direction. Who knows what these changes might lead to? Perhaps, it may culminate in a nuclear family system (Benoit, Levi & Vimard 1986). Perhaps the extended family structure will continue to play a dynamic role in Nigeria's urbanizing society (Oke 1986).

The problem of sexual promiscuity among teenagers is becoming a serious one. Because the authority of the parents has eroded, children take decisions on their own and do not feel accountable to anyone else. This case illustrates the pitiful situation of the Igala youth.

Case #4: **SEXUAL PROMISCUITY**

Joy was a young lady whose parents were Christians. She also professes to be a Christian. When she went to a government high school in a town about eighteen miles from home, she became free and traveled in the company of bad girls. She became promiscuous and was pregnant. Her desire not to drop out of school led her to abort the baby and she was excommunicated by her church.

Two years later, she began to flirt and became pregnant again. In her bid to abort this pregnancy she almost lost her life. They succeeded, however, in aborting the baby. Up till this time, she was still out of fellowship and did not show any sign of repentance.

A few months after the second abortion, she brought a young man to her parents' home and introduced him as her boyfriend. She also told her parents that she intended to marry the young man. Later the parents discovered that the young man was a married man and had children. When Joy's parents confronted her with the issue of marrying a family man, she told them that she would marry this man whether they gave their consent or not.

Although she has not yet married him, her own decision is the key issue here since she has refused to allow the parents to decide for her in this matter.

The Igala people are very religious. The head of the family is the head of the family spiritual worship. In Igala family structure, children are led in worship and are to be chaste and to refrain from obscenity and sexual promiscuity. These values have significantly eroded.

Economic problems have led adults and children alike into certain practices that were frowned upon many years ago. Family worship is neglected. Sacrifices have to be offered and this involves economic means to meet such religious obligations and demands. Unemployment has also compounded the problem.

Young girls are involved in sexually promiscuous behavior because of the economic gains, the money offered to them. It is sad to see students whose lives have been wrecked because of the economic hardship which drives them into prostitution. These students cannot proceed to higher institutions, either because they could not make it academically or do not have the means to pay.

It may be important to also point out that economic problems which led to migration and urbanization affect the morality and moral life of family members (Schapera 1971; Brown 1983).

CHANGES IN THE SOCIAL STRUCTURE

The changes occurring in Igala social structure are phenomenal. However, these changes are either accepted or tolerated for the economic benefits they bring to the people. The following changes are typical in the Igala contemporary society.

POLITICAL LEADERSHIP

Before the coming of the Europeans, Igala people were ruled and controlled by their kings. Their kingship was believed to be divine and people were to submit to the authority of the king. However, colonialism introduced the system of indirect rule in which subordinate officers were appointed to help the King or *Attah Igala. Attah Igala* is the title of the King of Igala and this title implies that he is the "Father" of the Igala people. In Igala contemporary society, there is a constitutional government which is democratic and egalitarian.

The traditional emphasis on royalty, family background, age and gender for political leadership has given way to the new democratic system of government. In the present system, economic power now determines who controls and assumes political leadership.

SOCIAL HIERARCHY

Social status was formally based on feudalism or slavery. The divine nature of Igala Kingship perpetuated the social hierarchy in which some people were looked upon as the superior while the rest were inferior. The emphasis was on whether on was *Oma Ojata* or *Oma Ofe* (of royal background). This practice has given way to the present where there are two classes of the upper and lower groups based essentially on the socio-economic status of individuals. As economic and political power now leads to political control, social stratification solely on the basis of aristocracy has become a thing of the past.

The process of social interaction has also changed with contemporary social hierarchy. Igala social activities in voluntary associations which were formally not open to all sexes and ages are changing. As people use their economic power to control, social involvement in voluntary organizations have been integrated to accommodate women and young people who have the means to influence opinions and power exchange.

INHERITANCE AND KINSHIP RELATIONS

In the traditional Igala society, children could not inherit directly from their parents. They were allowed to enjoy the right to use their parents' or grandparents' properties by the elders, who were either their parents or grandparents' siblings. Thus, inheritance among the Igala was based on the adelphic principle.

The customary law of inheritance is changing because kin allegiance is no longer respected as people become financially sound and independent. It is the practice for children to fight for the right to inherit their parents' or grandparents' properties today — which was formerly unheard of.

In the same way, the pattern of living is changing. People make their homes anywhere they choose or prefer as long as their interests are served. They care less about the feeling of their ancestors in this matter of inheritance and place of residence.

The traditional emphasis on group interest has been replaced with the interest of individuals. Because people have the economic means to influence others, they often get the cooperation and loyalty of people to sympathize with them.

APPLICATION: IMPLICATIONS FOR CHURCH PLANTING

The changes occurring in Igala society are affecting the family. The church must prepare to face the problems that these changes are creating and should not continue to remain indifferent to non-spiritual issues. She must stop ignoring major social and cultural problems that modernity has brought. The church planter must be realistic in his reaction to such social and cultural problems.

The cases recorded here show the transitional nature of contemporary Igala society. A holistic analysis of Igala family structure in these cases reveals that the Igala is experiencing cultural changes. Changes are constant and the people live with them. These are indications that the Igala people must be studied well in determining appropriate forms by which to reach them with the gospel.

In presenting the gospel to the Igala, close attention should be paid to the rapidity of changes in their society today. These changes may be frowned upon by the society but they are accepted and accommodated. Similarly, the gospel is bound to bring about changes in the lives of people. Instead of trying to confine people to their past practices, the gospel should be used to address their present, and guide them into the future. The missionaries cannot be held exclusively responsible for such changes, even though they are agents of change and are part of them.

Chapter Eight

CONCLUSION

The main thrust and focus of this book is that the church planter needs to be sensitive to the social structure of his receptors. He also needs to apply social structural insights to his church planting process in order that churches planted might be dynamically conditioned to their socio-cultural environments. This sensitivity to and application of insights from social structure should lead the churches themselves to desire to plant such dynamic equivalent churches wherever they minister.

According to Seamands, "Christian movement has taken a plant bred in North America or Europe and sought to transplant it to other soils. Conviction has grown in recent years that our mission is to sow the seed of the gospel and then allow it to grow according to the culture and soil of the land ... changes will take place, of course, but these should be brought about by the dynamics of the gospel and not the manipulation of the missionary" (Seamands, 1988:117). Many other missiological studies (Mayers, 1978; M. Kraft, 1978; C. Kraft, 1979; Murikwa, 1984; Iroezi, 1981; Hosense, 1980; Tienou, 1984 and Stotte, 1980) have identified this cultural imperialism in Third World missions. As Third World countries have begun to send missionaries for home and foreign cross-cultural ministries, they too face the problems for which Western missionaries have been traditionally blamed. These Third World missionaries are included in this admonition.

The argument of this book is that all those involved in church planting should be willing to relate their methods and strategies to the social structure of their receptors. As Seamands stresses, "the Christian message must be adapted to the cultural background of the listener in order to be more intelligible and effective" (Seamands, 1988:117). This writer in support argues that while restraint is called on church planters not to impose their own cultural baggage on their receptors, similar caution is necessary in adapting cultural values necessary for effective church planting ministry.

While this book shows the elements of social structure of the Igala of Central Nigeria, the writer presents the significance and indespensability of social structural issues to church planting process anywhere. Furthermore, the book demonstrates that Igala social structure is crucial to church planting among the Igala people; and that similar procedure by which social structural insights are gained and applied have general application to any cultural setting.

The procedure for utilizing social structural principles in church planting should involve or incorporate the following:

— Identification of social structure elements: This relates to the definition and delineation of issues which constitute a people's social structure. The church planter should be able to identify his receptors' social structural issues.

— Knowledge of social structure elements: It is not enough to identify the issues or elements, the church planter must proceed to study and know those issues well.

— Ability to relate social issues to church planting issues: The church planter needs to ask questions which would enable him to relate social structural issues to church planting questions and concerns.

— Application of social structural insights to missiological problems: After the church planter has known his social structure well, the next thing to do is to apply such knowledge in addressing the concerns or issues he faces in church planting process.

— Biblical appraisal of the application: The church planter

should allow the Bible to judge the cultural values or social structure of his receptors. It is significant for him to be sensitive to what the Bible is teaching his receptors and not his own understanding of the Bible in his own culture. He should allow and trust the Holy Spirit to bring about needed changes, thorough understanding and ultimate results.

The church planter is an instrument God uses to plant a church. The Holy Spirit, who is the agent of regeneration, has the ultimate power to bring about transformation. Whatever this writer has suggested or introduced should be looked upon as human method or strategy to make the instrument effective. Therefore, the Holy Spirit helping human instruments to understand God's Word and God's world of people should remain the church planter's ultimate source and point of reference. May He go ahead of us to plant His churches and may we remain His co-laborers!

BIBLIOGRAPHY

Aborampah, Osei-Mensah
1987 Plural Marriage and Fertility Differentials: A Study of Yoruba of Western Nigeria. Human Organization 46 (1):27-38

Adepegba, C. O.
1985 Context, Content, and Spirituality of Igbo Prayers. Research in African Literature 16 (Fall):319-348

Amobi, Nnamdi Ken
1980 Economics of Family Size: The Case of the Developing Economics of Kenya and Nigeria. City University of New York: Ph. D. dissertation.

Anyanwu, H. Onyema
1985 Why the Igbos Abandoned Their Gods. African Theological Journal 14 (2):91-99

Anyanwu, K. Chukwulozie
1984 The Meaning of Ultimate Reality in Igbo Cultural Experience. Ultimate Reality and Meaning 7(2): 84-101.

Apeh, John E.
1987 Analytical Study of Igala Worldview and the

Communication. Unpublished paper presented to the School of Intercultural Studies, Biola University.

Apeh, John E.
1988 Igala World Views and Contextualization. Ann Arbor, Michigan: University Microfilm International.

Argbe, Sunday Agbons
1984 Phenomenon of Prayer in African Traditional Religion. D. Miss. dissertation, Pasadena: Fuller Seminary.

Armstrong, Robert G.
1955 The Igala and Idoma-Speaking Peoples in Peoples of the Niger-Benue Confluence, Daryll Forde (ed). Ethnographic Survey of Africa: West Africa, Part X. London: International African Institute.

Barber, Karin
1982 Popular Reactions to the Petro-Naira. The Journal of Modern African Studies 20 (3):431-450.

Benoit, D., Levi, P. and Vimard, P.
1986 Household Structures in Rural Populations of South Togoland. Journal of Comparative Family Studies 17 (2):219-232.

Boston, John S.
1967 Igala in Encyclopedia Britannica.

Boston, John S.
1968 Oral Tradition and the History of Igala, Journal of African History, 10, no. 1:29-43.

Boston, John S.
1970 The Supernatural Aspect of Disease and Therapeutics Among the Igala. African Notes 5 (3):41-56.

Boston, John S.
1971 Medicines and Fetishes in Igala. Africa 41 (1971): 200-207.

Brown, Barbara
1983 The Impact of Male Labour Migration on Women in African Affairs 82 (328):367-388.

Burnett, David

1984 Cultural Factors and Indigenisation in Church Planting. In How to Plant Churches, edited by Monica Hill. London: MARC Europe.

Callaway, Barbara J.

1984 Ambiguous Consequences of the Socialization and Seclusion of Hausa Women. The Journal of Modern African Studies 22 (3):429-450.

Carstens, Peter

1982 The Socio-economic Context of Initiation Ceremonies Among Two Southern African Peoples. Canadian Journal of African Studies 16 (3):505-522.

Chalifonx, Jean-Jacques

1980 Secondary Marriage and Levels of Seniority Among the Abisi (PITI) Nigeria. Journal of Comparative Family Studies. XI:325-334.

Chiepe, G.K.T.

1985 Interview of Chiepe. Africa Report 30 (2):14-16.

Cotterell, Peter

1984 Cross-Cultural Church Planting: A Comment from the Field of Human Communications. In How to Plant Churches, edited by Monica Hill. London: MARC Europe.

Crane, William H.

1964 Indigenization in the African Church, International Review of Missions, 53 (1964):408-422.

Crowther, Samuel A.

1855 Journal of an Expedition up the Niger and Tshadda Rivers. 2nd ed. London:Church Missionary Society.

Culinovic, Vesna

1983 Changes of the Rural Family and in Wedding Customs. Sociologija Sela 21 (82):183-197.

Dahrenrendorf, Ralf

1963 Class and Class Conflict in Industrial Society. Stanford: Stanford University Press.

Davis, D.
1983 The Family and Social Change in the New Foundland Outport. Culture 3 (1):19-32.

Dillon, Malone C.
1983 The "Mutumwa" Churches of Zambia: An Indigenous African Religious Healing Movement. Journal of Religion in Africa 14 (3):204-222.

Douglas, Mary
1971 Is Matriliny Doomed? In Man in Africa. Edited by Douglas and P. Kaberry. New York: Doubleday-Anchor.

Due, Jean M. and Rebecca Summary
1982 Africana. The Journal of Modern African Studies 20 (1):155-166.

Duru, Mary S.
1984 Continuity in the Midst of Change: Underlying Themes in Igbo Culture. Anthropological Quarterly 56:1-9.

Emereuwaonu, Ernest U.
1977 Marital Fertility, Desired Family Size, Communication Channels and Modern Reproductive Values in an African City. University of California, Los Angeles: Ph.D. dissertation.

Ferrier, Mercia
1983 Sexism in Australian Cities: Barrier to Employment Opportunities. Women's Studies International Forum 6 (1):73-84.

Flanagan, William G.
1977 The Extended Family as an Agent in Urbanization: A Study of Men and Women Working in Dar es Salaam, Tanzania. The University of Connecticut: Ph.D. dissertation.

Foster, G.M.
1973 Traditional Societies and Technological Change. New York: Harper and Row Publishers.

Fosu, Gabrile B.
1986 Fertility and Family Planning in Accra. Journal of Biosocial Science 18 (1):11-22.

Hafkin, N. and E. Bay
1976 Women in Africa: Studies in Social and Economic Change. Stanford: Stanford University Press.

Hurskainen, Arvi
1985 Epistemiology of Spirit Possession Among the Maasai in Tanzania. African Theological Journal 14 (3): 161-173.

Kalu, Ogbu
1977 God in Retreat: Models of Religious Change in Africa. Nigerian Journal of the Humanities 1:42-53.

Kraft, Marguerite G.
1978 Worldview and the Communication of the Gospel: A Nigerian Case Study. Pasadena: William Carey Library.

Koji, Miyazaki
1983 Divination and Social Change in Java: Cultural Continuity and Discontinuity. Japanese Journal of Ethnology. 48 (2):129-145.

Kossoudji, Sherrie and Eva Jueller
1983 The Economic and Demographic Status of Female-headed Households in Rural Botswana. Economic Development and Cultural Change 31:(4):831-860.

Laslett, Peter and Richard Walls (eds.)
1972 Household and Family in Pastime. Cambridge: University Press.

Liker, Jeffrey K. and Glen H. Elder Jr.
1983 Economic Hardship and Marital Relations in the 1930's. American Sociological Review 48 (3):343-359.

Lingenfelter, Sherwood G.
1975 Yap: Political Leadership and Culture Change in an Island Society. Honolulu: The University Press of Hawaii.

Mann, K.
1981 Marriage Choices Among the Educated African Elites in Lagos, 1880-1915. International Journal of African Studies 14 (2):201-228.

Mann, K.
1983 Dangers of Dependence: Christian Marriage Among Elite Women in Lagos Colony, 1880-1915. Journal of African History 24 (1):37-56.

Marks, Shula and Richard Rathbone
1983 The History of the Family in Africa: Introduction. The Journal of African History 24 (2):145-161.

Marshall, L.B. and M. Marshall
1982 Education of Women and Family Size in Two Micronesian Communities. Micronesia 18 (1):1-22.

McCrea, Joan M.
1983 The Socio-Economic Role of Women in the People's Republic of China. Women's Studies International Forum 6 (1):57-72.

McKinney, Carol Virginia
1985 The Bajju of Central Nigeria: A Case Study of Religious and Social Change. Unpublished Doctoral Dissertation. Southern Methodist University, Dallas, Texas.

Mikell, Gwendolyn
1984 Filiation, Economic Crisis, and the Status of Women in Rural Ghana. Canadian Journal of African Studies 18 (1):195-218.

Morgan, Karen J., S.R. Johnson and James Burd (eds.)
1983 Household Size and the Cost of Nutritionally Equivalent Diets. American Journal of Public Health 73 (3):530-538.

Ngwisha, Kaluba John
1978 Urbanization and Family Structure: A Study of the Family on the Copperbelt of Zambia. Brandeis University: Ph.D. dissertation.

Nketia, J.
1982 On the Historicity of Music in African Cultures. Journal of African Studies (Fall): 90.

Oke, E. Adewale
1986 Kinship Interaction in Nigeria in Relation to Societal Modernization: A Pragmatic Approach. Journal of Comparative Family Studies 17 (2):185-196.

Okonjo, Isabel Kamene
1976 The Role of Women in Social Change Among the Igbo of Southeastern Nigeria Living West of the River Niger. Boston University Graduate School: Ph.D. dissertation.

Redfield, Robert
1956 The Little Community/Peasant Society and Culture. Chicago: University Press.

Rizika, Jill
1985 U.N. and Women: After the Decade. Africa Report 30 (5):75-81.

Rogombe, Rose F.
1985 Equal Partners in Africa's Development. Africa Report 30 (2):17-20.

Sacks, Karen H.B.
1971 Economic Bases of Sexual Equality: A Comparative Study of Four African Societies. The University of Michigan: Ph.D. Dissertation.

Schapera, Isaac
1971 Married Life in an African Tribe. Harmondsworth, NY: Penguin.

Schon, James F. and Samuel A. Crowther
1842 Journal of the ... Expedition Up the Niver in 1841. London: Hatchard. Second edition: 1970.

Seamands, John T.
1988 Harvest of Humanity. Wheaton, Illinois: Victor Books.

Seton, R.S.
1929-30 Notes on the Igala Tribe, Northern Nigeria, Journal of the African Society, 29:42-52, 149-163.

Shannon, L.W.
1979 The Changing Worldview of Minority Migrants in an Urban Setting. Human Organization 38 (1):52-62.

Shelton, Austin J.
1971 The Igbo-Igala Borderland. Albany: State University of New York Press.

Sieber, Roy
1965 The Insignia of the Igala Chief of Eteh, Eastern Nigeria Man 65, no.65: (May): 80-82.

Steady, Filomina Chioma
1985 African Women at the End of the Decade. Africa Report 30 (2):408.

Sudarkasa, Niara
1982 Sex Roles, Education and Development in Africa. Anthropology and Education Quarterly 13 (3):279-289.

Temple, C.L.(ed)
1919 Notes on the Tribes, Provinces, Emirates, and States of the Northern Provinces of Nigeria Compiled from Official Reports by O. Temple. Lagos: CMS Press. Reprint, London: F. Cass, 1965.

Tuladhar, J.M.
1985 Determinants of Contraceptive Use in Nepal. Journal of Biosocial Science 17 (2):185-193.

Ugwuegbu, Denis C.
1982 Effectiveness of Self-persuasion in Producing Healthy Attitudes Towards Polygymy. In Sex Roles Attitudes and Cultural Change, edited by Ira Gross, John Downing and Adma d'Heurle. Amsterdam, Holland: D. Reidel.

Ukpabi, S.C.
1965 Nsukka Before the Establishment of British Administration, Nksukka Division: A Geographical Appraisal, Parbati Sircar (ed). Nsukka: University of Nigeria, Annual Conference of the Nigerian Geographical Association Proceedings.

Uzoka, Azubike F.
1980 The African Child and the Dilemma of Changing Family Functions: A psychological perspective. African Social Research 30:851-867.

Vellenga, Dorothy Dee
1975 Changing Sex Roles and Social Tesions in Ghana: the Law as Measure and Mediator of Family Conflicts. Columbia University: Ph.D. dissertation.

Verma, K.K.
1984 Value of Children, Family Welfare and Communication Strategy: Some Observations. Journal of Social and Economic Review 1 (3):287-297.

Wyllie, Robert W.
1983 Ghanaian Spiritual and Traditional Healers Explanation of Illness: A Preliminary Survey. Journal of Religion in Africa. 14 (1):46-57.

Yonker, Dolores M.
1982 Dream as Validator in Traditional African Cultures. Dream Works. 1982, 2 (3):242-250.